# THE FACTS FACTORY

**Gyles Brandreth**

**Illustrated by
Rowan Barnes-Murphy**

**KNIGHT BOOKS**
Hodder and Stoughton

Copyright © Gyles Brandreth 1979
Illustrations Copyright © Hodder
and Stoughton 1979
First published by Knight Books 1979
*Second impression 1982*

British Library C.I.P.

Brandeth, Gyles
The Facts Factory
1. Children's encyclopedias and dictionaries
I. Title
082          AG5

ISBN 0 340 23477 6

_____

Printed and bound in Great Britain for
Hodder and Stoughton Paperbacks,
a division of Hodder and Stoughton Ltd.,
Mill Road, Dunton Green, Sevenoaks, Kent
(Editorial Office: 47 Bedford Square,
London, WC1 3DP), by
Hunt Barnard Printing Ltd.,
Aylesbury, Bucks.

# THE FACTS FACTORY

Be a fact-finder, with a visit to the many rooms of THE FACTS FACTORY.

Whether you're at school or at home, here's a handy pocket-sized encyclopaedia, simply bursting with fascinating information of all kinds.

Now you can have facts literally at your fingertips with all the knowledge produced by THE FACTS FACTORY's hot line!

*Jacket illustration by David Mostyn*

*A group of pigs is called a litter . . .*

Contents of

# THE FACTS FACTORY

*Room*          *Production Line*

Animals

# ENDANGERED ANIMALS

These are ten of the most endangered animals in the world.

| Species | Estimated number |
| --- | --- |
| Cheetah | 2,000 |
| European Bison | 700–800 |
| Fin Whale | 150,000 |
| Golden Lion Marmoset | under 400 |
| Hawaiian Goose | 500 |
| Indian Tiger | 2,600 |
| Japanese Crested Ibis | 8 |
| Polar Bear | 10,000–20,000 |
| Spanish Imperial Eagle | 100 |
| Whooping Crane | 59 |

# THE LIFE SPAN OF TEN DOMESTIC ANIMALS AND BIRDS

|  | Maximum recorded life in years |
|---|---|
| Budgerigar | 28 |
| Cat | 34 |
| Cow | 25 |
| Dog | 29 |
| Guinea Pig | 13½ |
| Hamster | 10 |
| Horse | 62 |
| Pig | 27 |
| Rabbit | 18 |
| Sheep | 20 |

# THE LIFE SPAN OF TEN WILD MAMMALS

|  | Maximum recorded life in years |
|---|---|
| Elephant | 70 |
| Fox | 14 |
| Hedgehog | 5 |
| Hippopotamus | 54 |
| Kangaroo | 16 |
| Lion | 29 |
| Monkey | 47 |
| Otter | 15 |
| Tiger | 22 |
| Whale | 90 |

## ANIMALS AND BIRDS IN GROUPS –
## AND WHAT TO CALL THEM

| | |
|---|---|
| Ants | Colony |
| Apes | Shrewdness |
| Badgers | Cete |
| Bass | Shoal |
| Bears | Sloth |
| Bees | Grist, Hive, Swarm |
| Birds | Flight |
| Boars | Singular, Sounder |
| Caterpillars | Army |
| Cats | Clowder, Clutter |
| Cattle | Drove |
| Chickens | Peep |

| | |
|---|---|
| Chicks | Brood, Clutch |
| Choughs | Chattering |
| Colts | Rag |
| Coots | Covert |
| Crows | Murder |
| Doves | Dule |
| Ducks | Balding |
| (on water) | Paddling |
| Eggs | Clutch |
| Elks | Gang |
| Finches | Charm |
| Fish | Draft, School |
| Foxes | Leash, Skulk |
| Geese (on water) | Gaggle |
| (in flight) | Skein |
| Gnats | Cloud, Horde |
| Goats | Tribe, Trip |
| Gorillas | Band |
| Hares | Down, Husk |
| Hawks | Cast |
| Hens | Brood |
| Herons | Siege |
| Horses | Harras |
| Hounds | Cry |
| Jellyfish | Smack |
| Kangaroos | Troop |
| Kittens | Kindle |
| Lapwings | Deceit |
| Larks | Exhaltation |
| Leopards | Leap |
| Lions | Pride |
| Locusts | Plague |
| Magpies | Tidings |
| Moles | Labor |
| Monkeys | Troop |
| Mules | Span |
| Nightingales | Watch |
| Owls | Parliament |

| | |
|---|---|
| Partridges | Covey |
| Peacocks | Muster |
| Pheasants | Covey |
| Pigs | Litter |
| Plovers | Congregations, Wing |
| Ponies | String |
| Pups | Litter |
| Rabbits | Colony |
| Ravens | Unkindness |
| Rhinoceroses | Crash |
| Rooks | Building |
| Seals | Pod |
| Sheep | Flock |
| Snipe | Walk |
| Sparrows | Host |
| Squirrels | Dray |
| Starlings | Murmuration |
| Storks | Mustering |
| Swallows | Flight |
| Swans | Bevy |
| Swine | Drift |
| Teals | Spring |
| Toads | Knot |
| Trout | Hover |
| Turkeys | Rafter |
| Turtledoves | Pitying |
| Turtles | Bale |
| Whales | Gam, Pod |
| Widgeon | Company |
| Wildfowl | Plump |
| Wolves | Route |
| Woodpeckers | Descent |

# TEN OF THE WORLD'S LARGEST ANIMALS

African Elephant – The African elephant can weigh as much as 6 tonnes and is consequently the largest land animal.

Anaconda – The largest and heaviest of all snakes, the Anaconda can weigh nearly 227 kg and measure over 8.5 metres long.

Blue Whale – This is probably the largest animal that ever lived and it is certainly the largest animal in the world today. It has been known to grow to a length of almost 30 metres and can weigh up to 160 tonnes.

Giant Salamander – The Giant Salamander is found in Japan. It is the largest living amphibian and can reach a length of 1.8 metres.

Giant Squid – This is the largest animal without a backbone.

Giraffe – Tallest of all animals the Giraffe can grow to a height of 5.7 metres.

Hercules Moth – As its name suggests, the Hercules Moth has unusual qualities. It is, in fact, the largest moth in the world, with a wing span of 36 cm.

Ostrich – Although it cannot fly the Ostrich is quite capable of protecting itself on the ground. Weighing over 90 kg, Ostriches have been known to grow to a height of 2.4 metres.

Stick Insect – The Stick Insect is the longest of all insects, measuring up to 45 cm long.

Whale Shark – The largest fish in the sea, the Whale Shark may be up to 13.6 metres long.

Big, Big, Big

# THE WORLD'S TOP TEN ISLANDS

These are the ten largest islands in the world.

| Island | Ocean or Sea | Area (km²) |
|---|---|---|
| *(Australia) | | 7,618,493 |
| Greenland | Arctic Ocean | 2,175,600 |
| New Guinea | Pacific Ocean | 777,000 |
| Borneo | Indian Ocean | 725,545 |
| Madagascar | Indian Ocean | 590,000 |
| Baffin Island | Arctic Ocean | 476,065 |
| Sumatra | Indian Ocean | 473,600 |
| Honshū (Japan) | Pacific Ocean | 228,000 |
| Great Britain | Atlantic Ocean | 218,041 |
| Victoria Island | Arctic Ocean | 212,197 |
| Ellesmere Island | Arctic Ocean | 196,236 |

*(Australia is geographically regarded as a continental land mass, like America.)

# THE WORLD'S TOP TEN CITIES

According to population estimates, these are the ten largest cities in the world.

| | |
|---|---|
| TOKYO, Japan | 11,581,000 |
| SHANGHAI, China | 10,820,000 |
| MEXICO CITY, Mexico | 10,223,000 |
| NEW YORK, USA | 9,739,000 |
| PARIS, France | 8,424,000 |
| BUENOS AIRES, Argentina | 8,353,000 |
| SÃO PAOLO, Brazil | 7,594,000 |
| PEKING, China | 7,570,000 |
| MOSCOW, USSR | 7,410,000 |
| LONDON, UK | 7,168,000 |

# TEN OF THE WORLD'S BIGGEST CONSTRUCTIONS

| Construction | Location | Size or Capacity |
|---|---|---|
| Breakwater | Los Angeles, USA | 13.29 km long |
| Chimney | Ontario, Canada | 379.6 m high |
| Dry Dock | Nagasaki, Japan | 970 m x 100 m x 14.5 m |
| Garage | Chicago, USA | 9,250 cars |
| Hotel | Moscow, USSR | 3,200 rooms |
| Library | Washington D.C., USA | 73,000,000 items |
| Refinery (oil) | Amuya Bay, Venezuela | 32,000,000 tonnes |
| Stadium | Prague, Czechoslovakia | 240,000 spectators |
| Vat | Hereford, England | 74,099 hectolitres |
| Wall | China | 6,320 km long |

Continents & Countries

# THE EARTH

| | |
|---|---|
| Total Surface Area (estimated) | 510,066,100 km² |
| Land Area | 148,328,000 km² |
| Water Area | 361,740,000 km² |
| Equatorial Circumference | 40,075.03 km |
| Meridian Circumference | 40,007.89 km |
| Equatorial Diameter | 12,756.280 km |
| Polar Diameter | 12,713.510 km |
| Centre of the Earth | Almost 6,440 km beneath our feet |

# THE SEVEN CONTINENTS

|  | Area (km²) |
|---|---|
| Asia | 44,011,000 |
| America | 42,043,000 |
| North America | 21,500,000 |
| Central America | 2,750,000 |
| South America | 17,793,000 |
| Africa | 30,232,000 |
| Antarctica | 13,600,000 |
| Europe (includes all territory of the USSR west of the Ural mountains) | 10,523,000 |
| Oceania (includes part of Irian Jaya, politically in Asia) | 8,935,000 |

# THE COUNTRIES OF THE COMMONWEALTH

| | |
|---|---|
| Australia | Malta |
| Bahamas | Mauritius |
| Bangladesh | Nauru |
| Barbados | New Zealand |
| Botswana | Nigeria |
| Canada | Papua New Guinea |
| Cyprus | Seychelles |
| Fiji | Sierra Leone |
| Gambia | Singapore |
| Ghana | Sri Lanka |
| Grenada | Swaziland |
| Guyana | Tanzania |
| India | Tonga |
| Jamaica | Trinidad and Tobago |
| Kenya | Uganda |
| Lesotho | United Kingdom |
| Malawi | Western Samoa |
| Malaysia | Zambia |

*Dependencies and Associated States*

Australia:
 Australian Antarctic
  Territory
 Christmas Island
 Cocos (Keeling)
  Island
 Coral Sea Islands
  Territory
 Norfolk Island
New Zealand:
 Cook Islands
 Niue Island
 Ross Dependency
 Tokelau
United Kingdom:
 Antigua
 Belize
 Bermuda
 British Antarctic
  Territory
 British Indian Ocean
  Territory
 British Virgin Islands
 Brunei
 Canton and Enderbury
  Islands (United
  Kingdom – United
  States
  Condominium)

Cayman Islands
Channel Islands
Dominica
Falkland Islands
Falkland Islands
 Dependencies
Gibraltar
Gilbert Islands
Hong Kong
Isle of Man
Montserrat
New Hebrides
Pitcairn Islands
St. Christopher-
 Nevis-Anguilla
St. Helena
 Ascension
 Tristan da Cunha
St. Lucia
St. Vincent
Solomon Islands
Turks and Caicos
 Islands
Tuvalu
(Rhodesia is still legally
 under British
 sovereignty)

# THE COUNTRIES OF THE EUROPEAN COMMUNITY

Belgium
Denmark
France
Germany
Ireland
Italy
Luxembourg
Netherlands
United Kingdom

# Data

# METRIC MEASURES AND THEIR IMPERIAL EQUIVALENTS

## Length

| | |
|---|---|
| 1 centimetre (cm) = 10 millimetres (mm) | 0.3937 in. |
| 1 metre (m) = 100 centimetres | 1.094 yd. |
| 1 kilometre (km) = 1,000 metres | 0.62137 mile |

(A kilometre is approximately five-eighths of a mile, so that 8 kilometres may be regarded as 5 miles.)

## Surface or Area

| | |
|---|---|
| 1 sq. centimetre = 100 sq. mm | 0.155 sq. in. |
| 1 sq. metre = 10,000 sq. cm | 1,196 sq. yd. |
| 1 are = 100 sq. m | 119.6 sq. yd. |
| 1 hectare = 100 ares | 2.4711 acres |
| 1 sq. kilometre = 100 hectares | 0.386103 sq. mile |

## Capacity

| | |
|---|---|
| 1 cu. centimetre | 0.061 cu. in. |
| 1 cu. metre = 999.972 litres | 1.30795 cu. yd. |
| 1 litre = 1.000028 cu. dm. | 1.7598 pint |

(Cu. dm. is the abbreviation for cubic decimetre.)

## Weight

| | |
|---|---|
| 1 milligram (mg) | 0.015 grain |
| 1 gramme (g) = 1,000 milligrams | 15.432 grains |
| 1 kilogram (kg) = 1,000 grammes | 2.2046 lb. |
| 1 quintal = 100 kilograms | 1.968 cwt. |
| 1 tonne = 10 quintals | 0.9842 ton |

# IMPERIAL MEASURES AND THEIR METRIC EQUIVALENTS

*length*

| | |
|---|---|
| 1 inch | 2.54 cm |
| 1 foot = 12 inches | 0.3048 m |
| 1 yard = 3 feet | 0.9144 m |
| 1 chain = 4 rods = 22 yards | 20.1168 m |
| 1 mile = 8 furlongs = 80 chains | 1.6093 km |
| 1 nautical mile = 6,080 feet | 1.852 km |

*Surface or Area*

| | |
|---|---|
| 1 sq. inch | 6.4516 sq. cm |
| 1 sq. foot = 144 sq. inch | 9.2903 sq. dm |
| 1 sq. yard = 9 sq. feet | 0.836 sq. m |
| 1 acre = 4 roods = 4,840 sq. yards | 4,046.556 sq. m |
| 1 sq. mile = 640 acres | 258.99 hectares |

*Capacity*

| | |
|---|---|
| 1 cu. inch | 16.387 cu. cm |
| 1 cu. foot = 1,728 cu. inch | 28.317 cu. du |
| 1 cu. yard = 27 cu. feet | 0.7646 cu. m |
| 1 pint = 4 gills | 0.568 litres |
| 1 gallon = 4 quarts = 8 pints | 4.546 litres |
| 1 bushel = 4 pecks = 8 gallon | 36.368 litres |

*Weight*

| | |
|---|---|
| 1 ounce = 16 drams = 437.5 grains | 28.35 gm |
| 1 pound = 16 ounces | 0.4536 kg |
| 1 stone = 14 pounds | 6.35 kg |
| 1 hundredweight = 4 quarters = 8 stones | 0.5080 quintal |
| 1 ton = 20 hundredweight | 1.016 tonnes |

# MATHEMATICAL SIGNS

There are many signs used in mathematics, but this is what the main ones mean.

| Sign | Meaning |
|---|---|
| $=$ | is equal to |
| $\neq$ | Is not equal to |
| $\simeq$ | Is approx. equal to |
| $\equiv$ | Is identical to |
| $\backsim$ | The difference between |
| $\propto$ | Varies as |
| $>$ | Greater than |
| $\ngtr$ | Not greater than |
| $<$ | Less than |
| $\nless$ | Not less than |
| $\Sigma$ | The sum of |
| $\delta$ | A small difference |
| $\angle$ | Angle |
| $\infty$ | Infinity |

60 seconds (″) = 1 minute (′)
60 minutes = 1 degree (°)
90 degrees = 1 right angle
4 right angles = 1 circle (360°)

# FAHRENHEIT AND CENTIGRADE

Gabriel Daniel Fahrenheit (1688–1736) was a German physicist who made important improvements in the construction of thermometers and introduced the thermometric scale known by his name. It has a boiling point at 212° and a freezing point at 32°.

The Centigrade thermometer was invented by Anders Celsius (1701–1744), a Swedish astronomer. The Celsius scale has a boiling point at 100° and a freezing point at 0° (zero).

To convert Fahrenheit into Centigrade: subtract 32, multiply by 5 and divide by 9.
To convert Centigrade into Fahrenheit: multiply by 9, divide by 5 and add 32.

# EARLY MEASUREMENTS

In the ancient world and even in the middle ages men were accustomed to using their limbs as measures. Many of these measures have been standardised and some are still in use today. Here are ten of the most common:

Cubit – A cubit is the length of a man's forearm, about 45 cm long, and is often referred to in the Bible.

Digit – A digit is the width of a man's finger. The word comes from the Latin word for a finger 'digitus'.

Foot – There are no prizes for guessing how this got its name. It was later standardised to a length of 12 inches, 30 cm.

Hand – Originally a hand was the width of a hand or a palm, but it became standardised to 4 inches and is used for measuring the height of horses.

Inch – To begin with an inch was the width of a man's thumb. In the fourteenth century, however, Edward II decreed that an inch was to be the length of three grains of barley (barleycorns) laid end to end.

Mile – A mile is a shortened form for 'mille passuum', two Latin words which mean '1,000 paces'. It later became standardised as 1,760 yards.

Pace – Taken from a man's stride, one pace is approximately 76 cm long.

Rod – A rod is a measurement used in surveying. Apparently the unit was set in the sixteenth century by sixteen men placing their left feet one behind the other.

Span – A span is the distance from the end of the thumb to the end of the little finger when the hand is spread out, a little under 23 cm.

Yard – In the twelfth century the distance of one yard was set by Henry II. He decreed that it should be the distance from the end of his nose to the end of his thumb, when his arm was fully stretched out.

Acre – One acre was originally the width of a team of eight oxen. It measured one furlong long and four furrows wide.

B.T.U. – The British Thermal Unit (B.T.U.) is the amount of heat required to raise the temperature of 1 lb. (453 grams) of water by 1°F, (100,000 B.T.U. = 1 Therm).

Cable – The cable is a measurement of length used at sea and is equal to 240 yds. (219.35 m).

Furlong – Furlong is short for 'furrow long'. It was the distance a team of oxen could plough before needing a rest.

Gallon – One gallon of water weighs 10 lb. (4.53 kg).

Gramme – One gramme is the weight of 1 cc of pure water.

Horse-power – One horse-power is the amount of power needed to raise 550 lb. (249.48 kg) 1 ft. (30.48 cm) in 1 second.

Link – The link is a unit of length used in surveying. It is one hundredth part of a chain, or 7.92 inches (20.11 cm).

Litre – One litre is 1,000 cc of pure water and it weighs 1 kg.

Quire – One quire is 24 sheets of paper. 20 quires makes 1 ream.

## Exploration

MAJOR JOURNEYS OF EXPLORATION AND DISCOVERY

| | | |
|---|---|---|
| B.C. 700 | Phoenician and Carthaginian traders | Explored Mediterranean and adjacent coasts. |
| 450 | Hanno (Carthaginian) | Led 60 fifty-oared ships round the African coast as far as Sierra Leone. |
| 330–323 | Alexander the Great (Macedonian) | Marched through Persia to India and back to Babylon. |
| 325 | Pytheas (Greek) | Sailed from Marseille to North Sea coasts. |
| 200–100 | Romans | Penetrated up the Nile and reached the Baltic Sea. |

| A.D. 1–50 | Buddhist monks and traders | First reached China on the trade routes of Central Asia. |
| 867 | Norsemen | Discovered Iceland. |
| 982 | Eric the Red (Viking) | Discovered Greenland. |
| 1000 | Leif Ericsson (Viking) | Reached North America (Newfoundland). |
| 1253–5 | Guillaume de Rubruquis (French) | Journeyed through Crimea, Caucasus, Mongolia, Asia Minor |
| 1255 | Nicolo and Maffeo Polo (Venetian) | Reached Peking. |
| 1271 | Marco Polo (Venetian) | Journeyed through Asia. |
| 1325–54 | Ibn Batutu (Arab) | Journeyed from Tangiers via Mecca and Persia around the shores of the Indian and Pacific Oceans to China. |

| 1300s | João Zarco and Tristão Vas (Portuguese) | Discovered Madeira and the Azores. |
|---|---|---|
| 1487–8 | Bartholomew Diaz (Portuguese) | Rounded Cape of Good Hope. |
| 1492–6 | Christopher Columbus (Italian) | Discovered San Salvador Antigua, Bahamas, Cuba, Guadeloupe, Haiti, Jamaica, Montserrat and Puerto Rico. |
| 1497 | John Cabot (Genoese) | Discovered Cape Breton Island, Newfoundland and Nova Scotia. |
| 1496–1503 | Amerigo Vespucci (Florentine) | Explored Mexico and parts of the east coast of Central and South America. |
| 1498 | Vasco da Gama (Portuguese) | Discovered sea-route from Europe to India, round the Cape of Good Hope. |
| 1498 | Christopher Columbus (Italian) | Landed in South America. |
| 1499 | Vincente Pinzon (Portuguese) | Discovered Brazil and the Amazon. |
| 1501–61 | Various Portuguese Navigators | Discovered Canton, Ceylon, Goa, Japan, Malacca and the Islands of the East Indies. |
| 1502–4 | Christopher Columbus (Italian) | Discovered Trinidad. |
| 1509 | Sebastian Cabot (Genoese) | Explored America's east coast from Florida to mouth of River Plate. |
| 1513 | Vasco Nunez de Balboa (Spanish) | Crossed Panama Isthmus and sighted Pacific Ocean. |
| 1520 | Hernando Cortés (Spanish) | Conquered Mexico. |

| | | |
|---|---|---|
| 1519–22 | Ferdinand Magellan (Portuguese) | Sailed round the World, discovering Magellan Strait and the Philippine Islands. |
| 1534–6 | Jaques Cartier (French) | Discovered Canada and explored St Lawrence River. |
| 1539 | De Soto (Spanish) | Discovered Florida, Georgia and River Mississippi. |
| 1554 | Hugh Willoughby and Richard Chancellor (English) | Discovered the White Sea and sea-route to Russia. |
| 1557 | Francis Drake (English) | Sailed round the World in the Golden Hind. |
| 1576 | Martin Frobisher (English) | Started search for the North-West Passage to the Pacific. |
| 1587 | John Davis (English) | Discovered Davis Strait between Atlantic and Arctic Oceans. |
| 1594–97 | Willem Barentz (Dutch) | Explored seas north of Norway for a North East Passage. First to winter in the far north. |
| 1606 | William Janszoon (Dutch) | Discovered Australia. |
| 1606 | John Smith (British) | Explored Chesapeake Bay discovering Potomac and Susquehannah. |
| 1611 | Henry Hudson (British) | Sought North-East and North-West Passages and discovered Hudson Bay, River and Strait. |
| 1615 | William Baffin (British) | Explored Baffin Bay and Baffin Island while searching for the North-West Passage. |

| | | |
|---|---|---|
| 1642–4 | Abel Tasman (Dutch) | Discovered Fiji, New Zealand, Tasmania and Tonga. |
| 1661–64 | John Grueber and Albert d'Orville (Papal Explorers) | Journeyed from Peking to Rome through northern India and Middle East. (First Europeans to visit Lhasa, Tibet.) |
| 1700 | William Dampier (British) | Explored west coast of Australia. |
| 1728 | Vitus Bering (Danish) | Discovered Bering Strait between Asia and America. |
| 1740–4 | George Anson (British) | Sailed round the World in the Centurion. |
| 1767 | Samuel Wallis (British) | Discovered Tahiti. |
| 1768–71 | James Cook (British) | Sailed round the World in the Endeavour, charting the coast of New Zealand and the east coast of Australia. |
| 1772–6 | James Cook (British) | Discovered (in two further voyages) Cook Is., Easter Is., New Caledonia, Norfolk Is., and Hawaiian Is. |
| 1795–7 | Mungo Park (British) | Followed course of River Niger. |
| 1819–22 | Fabian Gottlieb von Bellings (Russian) | Circumvented Antarctica and made the first land sightings in the Antarctic Circle. |
| 1821–3 | James Weddell (British) | Discovered South Orkneys and Weddell Sea. |
| 1822–5 | Hugh Clapperton, Dixon Denham and Walter Oudney (British) | Expedition through Sudan to Lake Chad |

| | | |
|---|---|---|
| 1827–8 | René Caillié (French) | Crossed north-west Africa from Sierra Leone to Tangiers via Timbuktu. |
| 1828–45 | Charles Sturt (British) | Followed Darling and Murray Rivers and penetrated central Australia beyond Lake Eyre. |
| 1831 | James Clark Ross and John Ross (British) | Located North Magnetic Pole. |
| 1831–32 | John Biscoe (British) | Discovered part of Antarctica. |
| 1839–40 | Charles Wilkes (American) | Explored various Pacific islands and what is now Wilkes Land in Antarctica. |
| 1839–43 | James Clark Ross (British) | Discovered Mounts Erebus and Terror, Ross Ice Barrier and Victoria Land (Antarctica). |
| 1849–73 | David Livingstone (British) | Followed the course of the River Zambesi and discovered Victoria Falls and Lake Nyasa. |
| 1856 | John Speke (British) | Discovered Lake Tanganyika. |
| 1858 | John Speke (British) | Discovered Lake Victoria Nyanza. |
| 1860–61 | Robert O'Hara Burke (Irish) | Led the first south-north crossing of Australia. |

| | | |
|---|---|---|
| 1862 | John Speke and J. A. Grant (British) | Discovered source of the White Nile. |
| 1864 | Samuel Baker (British) | Discovered Lake Alberta Nyanza. |
| 1869–74 | Gustav Nachtigal (Germany) | Crossed North Africa from Tripoli, via Fezzan and Bornu to Cairo. |
| 1870–2 | Henry Stanley (British) | Met and explored with David Livingstone. |
| 1872–4 | Julius von Prayer and K. Weyfrecht (Bohemian) | Discovered Franz Josef Land. |
| 1874–7 | Henry Stanley (British) | Followed course of River Congo. |
| 1886–87 | Francis Younghusband (British) | Explored Manchuria and journeyed from Peking to Simla, through the Mustagh Pass. |
| 1890–1909 | Sven Hedin (Swiss) | Journeyed through Central Asia to Tibet and China. |
| 1901 | Robert Falcon Scott (British) | Discovered King Edward VII Land. |
| 1903–6 | Roald Amundsen (Norwegian) | First navigated the North-West Passage. |
| 1909 | Robert Peary (American) | Reached North Pole. |
| 1911 | Roald Amundsen (Norwegian) | Reached South Pole (Dec 14). |
| 1912 | Robert Falcon Scott (British) | Reached South Pole (Jan 18). |
| 1953 | Edmund Hillary (NZ) and Sherpa Tensing (Nepal) | Climbed Mount Everest. |

| 1957 | Vivian Fuchs (British) and Edmund Hillary (NZ) | Crossed Antarctic continent via South Pole. |
| 1968–9 | Wally Herbert, Alan Gill, Roy Koerner, Ken Hedges (British) | Crossed Arctic Ocean via North Pole. |
| 1969 | Neil Armstrong and Edwin Aldrin (American) | First men to walk on the Moon. |
| 1975 | British Expedition led by Christian Bonington | Climbed the south-west face of Mount Everest. |

Faster + Faster

# FASTEST INDIVIDUAL ACHIEVEMENTS

These are ten of the fastest individual achievements ever measured.

| Activity | Name and Nation | Speed |
|---|---|---|
| Amputation (leg) | D. Larrey (France) | 13–15 sec. |
| Cycling | A. V. Abbott (USA) | 226.1 km/h |
| Marathon Running | D. Clayton (Australia) | 16.30 km/h |
| Parachuting (free fall) | J. W. Kittinger (USA) | 988 km/h |
| Shorthand | N. Behrin (USA) | 350 w.p.m. |
| Skate Boarding | Richard K. Brown | 115.53 km/h |
| Speaking | R. Glendenning (GB) | 176 words in 30 sec. |
| Typing (manual machine) | M. Owen (USA) | 170 words in 1 minute |
| Walking on hands | T. P. Hunt | 45.72 m (50 yd.) in 19.1 sec. |
| Writing (novels) | C. Hamilton (alias Frank Richards [GB]) | 80,000 words a week. |

# FASTEST MACHINES AND MEANS OF TRANSPORT IN THE WORLD

| | |
|---|---|
| Aircraft | 3,529.56 km/h |
| Boat | 527.8 km/h |
| Car (powered by rockets) | 1,016 km/h |
| Computer | $9.78 \times 10^8$ results per second |
| Glider | 322 km/h |
| Helicopter | 557.8 km/h |
| Hydroplane | 556 km/h |
| Lift (passenger) | 36.56 km/h |
| Monorail (unmanned) | 4,972 km/h |
| Hovercraft (tracked) | 378 km/h |
| Motor Cycle | 495.183 km/h |
| Sailing Boat | 66.78 km/h |
| Space Capsule | 39,897 km/h |
| Train | 410 km/h |

# FASTEST PEOPLE IN SPORT

These are some of the fastest sportsmen ever recorded.

| Sport | Name and Nation | Speed |
|---|---|---|
| Boxing (punching) | S. R. Robinson (USA) | 56.00 km/h |
| Cricket (bowling) | J. R. Thompson (Australia) | 160.45 km/h |
| Ice Hockey (hitting the puck) | B. Hull (Canada) | 189.00 km/h |
| Ice skating | Y. Kulikov (USSR) | 47.36 km/h |
| Roller skating | G. Cantarella (Italy) | 41.48 km/h |
| Running | R. Hayes (USA) | 44.88 km/h |
| Skiing | Steve McKinney (USA) | 200.222 km/h |
| Swimming | Joe Bottom (USA) | 7.92 km/h |

| Tennis (service) | W. T. Tilden (USA) | 263.00 km/h |
| Tobogganing | P. Berchtold (Switzerland) | 145.00 km/h |
| Walking | B. Kannenberg (W. Germany) | 14.24 km/h |
| Water skiing | D. Churchill (USA) | 202.27 km/h |

## THE TEN FASTEST MAMMALS ON EARTH

| *Name* | *Maximum recorded speed in km/h* |
| --- | --- |
| Cheetah | 101.37 |
| Antelope | 98.15 |
| Gazelle | 80.46 |
| Hare | 72.41 |
| Kangaroo | 72.41 |
| Horse (mounted) | 69.60 |
| Dog (Saluki) | 69.19 |
| Deer | 67.59 |
| Zebra | 64.37 |
| Wolf | 57.93 |

# Gymnosperms.

Gymnosperm is the name given, in Natural History, to one of the divisions of plants. It comes from the Greek word 'gúmnos' which means 'naked' and is used to classify seed-bearing plants which carry their seeds exposed, usually in cones, instead of protecting them inside a fruit. The plants which do carry their seeds inside their fruit are classed as Angiosperms, from the Greek word 'aggêion' meaning a 'container'. Here are the names of the most important tree families which are found in these two divisions.

*Gymnosperms*

Cyatheacae – Tree ferns:

The spores drop off and grow into little flat plants which themselves produce spores from which another fern tree grows.

Ginkgoaceae – Ginkgo family:

This family has the oldest 'genus' (group of similar species) of tree still in existence. It is 100,000,000 years old.

Taxaceae – Yew family:

These are typical conifer trees, the flowers grow into open-ended cones resembling berries.

Cupressaceae – Cypress family:

The tiny leaves are pressed close to the twigs. The cones are small and round, beginning soft and fleshy they later become woody as they ripen.

Taxodiaeceae – Swamp cypress family:

Their narrow leaves are shaped into a spiral formation, the cones are round with leathery or woody scales on the surface.

Pinaceae – Pine family:

These trees have narrow leaves which are also arranged in spirals, though they are occasionally found in tufts or rows as well. Each scale of the woody cone has two seeds.


*Angiosperms*

Magnoliaceae – Magnolia family:

The flowers develop into a cone-like mass of seeds.

Fagaceae – Beech family:

The fruit is surrounded by a cup of woody texture.

Salicaceae – Willow family:

The flowers are in the form of catkins and the fruit is a capsule filled with lots of hairy seeds.

Rosaceae – Rose family:

The flowers are normally divided into five parts and the leaves have tiny leaflets at the base.

Leguminosae – Pea family:
   The flowers are irregular in shape and usually consist of five petals. The fruit is in the form of a pod containing two or more seeds.

Aceraceae – Maple family:
   Winged nutlets form the fruit of these trees and the leaves are positioned opposite each other on the twig.

Myrtaceae – Myrtle family:
   The flowers are formed in clusters with the fruit appearing as either a berry, drupe or capsule.

Oleaceae – Olive family:
   The flowers normally have four petals and two stamens. The fruits vary from the drupes of the olive to the winged nuts found on the ash.

Palaceae – Palms:
   Palms have uniform stems which end in a spiral of divided leaves. The mature seed is often large, as in the case of the coconut palm.


# FORESTS OF EUROPE AND NORTH AMERICA

These are the percentages of land under forest in ten countries on either side of the Atlantic and the proportions of Coniferous forest to Deciduous forest in these countries.

| Country | Land under forest | Coniferous forest | Deciduous forest |
| --- | --- | --- | --- |
| Austria | 33% | 86% | 14% |
| Canada | 23% | 61% | 39% |
| Finland | 64% | 81% | 19% |
| France | 22% | 46% | 54% |
| Germany, West | 28% | 71% | 29% |
| Greece | 18% | 48% | 52% |
| Italy | 20% | 45% | 55% |
| Sweden | 57% | 85% | 15% |
| United Kingdom | 7% | 54% | 46% |
| United States | 21% | 71% | 29% |

# GROWTH RATES OF TWENTY-FOUR COMMON TREES

Cedar of Lebanon – The Cedar of Lebanon is a fast growing tree which can appear very old and well established after only a hundred years.

Douglas fir – In the right conditions this tree can grow at the rate of nearly 1 metre a year from five to thirty-five, after that age it grows less quickly and the trunk thickens.

English elm – A strong, rapid growing tree which appears older than its actual age. After only one hundred years the tree can appear two or even three hundred years old.

English holly – A slow starter, it takes fifteen years for the holly to first send out shoots 50 cm long in one season.

English yew – Like the English holly the yew is a very slow grower, it grows as wide as it is high so that in the end its width is greater than its height.

European ash – Slower than the American ash, the English variety nevertheless reaches a height of 30.5 metres before it is one hundred years old.

European beech – Although it grows slowly in its first ten years the beech speeds up between the ages of ten and thirty, reaching its full maturity when it is one hundred years old, with its height and its width virtually the same dimension.

European larch – This is one of the quickest growing conifers. By the age of fifteen it is growing by almost 1 metre a year until it matures after one hundred years of growth.

European juniper – A very slow growing variety, the juniper barely reaches tree stature in one hundred years.

Holm oak – Despite starting slowly (it only grows 3 metres in ten years), the holm oak reaches a height of about 12 metres after thirty years. It only doubles its height in the following seventy years but its width increases considerably.

Horse chestnut – Growing at about 0.6 metres each year the horse chestnut reaches its full height after fifty or sixty years. After that time it spreads but grows no higher.

Lombardy poplar – For the first twenty-five years the lombardy poplar grows between 0.6 and 0.9 metres a year, after that time the rate of growth slows down.

London plane – Although it grows slower than the American plane this tree usually grows 0.6 metres a year during its early life.

Monterey pine – This is one of the fastest growing trees.

It will normally grow between 0.9 and 1.2 metres a year, but it has been known to grow as much as 6 metres in one year.

Roble beech – The Roble beech is one of the fastest growing broadleaves, reaching a height of 18 metres after only 15 years.

Scarlet oak – In the right conditions this is one of the fastest growing oaks, which can reach a height of 21 metres in a hundred years.

Scots pine – After the first three or four years the Scots pine grows rapidly but after losing its upward vigour it spreads and it is usually about 25 metres high by the time it is a hundred.

Serbian spruce – Growing in a slim spire shape the Serbian spruce increases its height by about 0.6 metres each year, reaching a height of 30 metres after a hundred years.

Silver birch – Despite its quick start this tree slows down after twenty years and is a little over 22 metres high at the age of a hundred.

Spanish chestnut – The Spanish chestnut grows fastest in its middle years, when it can send out shoots 3 metres long each year, arriving at a height of nearly 33 metres.

Swamp cypress – A slow steady grower, the Swamp cypress is still not fully matured by the time it is a hundred years old when it is usually slightly over 24 metres high.

Weeping willow – Growing and spreading at the same rate, the Weeping Willow is frequently 9 metres high and the same distance wide by the time it is fifteen years old.

Wellingtonia – This tree grows at a steady rate of 0.6–0.9 metres a year over a period of forty or fifty years, but tends to slow down as it approaches a height of 30 metres.

White willow – This is one of the fastest growing trees. It is so big by the age of thirty that it looks at least twice its age.

Higher & Higher

# THE LAYERS OF THE ATMOSPHERE

| Layer | Height | Description |
| --- | --- | --- |
| Exosphere | 500 km and above | The fifth layer and the beginning of space. |
| Thermosphere | 85 km – 500 km | The fourth layer of the atmosphere, with great variation in conditions between night and day. |

| | | |
|---|---|---|
| Mesosphere | 50 km – 85 km | The third layer of the atmosphere characterised by a significant drop in temperature with altitude. |
| Stratosphere | Upper limit of Troposphere – 50 km | The second layer of the atmosphere, with temperature increasing with altitude. |
| Troposphere | Surface level – 17 km (over equator), 6–8 km over the poles | The region of clouds and rain immediately above the land (lithosphere) and the sea (hydrosphere). |

## CLOUD LAYERS

| Type | Height of cloud base in metres | Description |
|---|---|---|
| Cirrus | 5,000–13,700 | Detached, delicate pieces of cloud with wispy appearance resembling hair. |
| Cirrocumulus | 5,000–13,700 | Round fleecy clouds in groups or rolls joined together forming what is often called a 'mackerel sky'. |

| | | |
|---|---|---|
| Cirrostratus | 5,000–13,700 | Sheets of cloud with a thin 'milky' appearance. |
| Altocumulus | 2,000–7,000 | Small, thin patches of rounded cloud, either very close or almost joined together. |
| Altostratus | 2,000–7,000 | Sheet or veil of cloud which can be either thick or thin. |
| Nimbostratus | 900–3,000 | Dark grey cloud sometimes trailing, which brings continuous rain or snow. |
| Stratocumulus | 460–2,000 | Round masses or rolls of cloud forming a layer or sheet, often close enough together for their edges to join. |
| Stratus | surface – 460 | Continuous grey layer of cloud sometimes giving drizzle. |
| Cumulus | 460–2,000 | Flat base with rounded masses piled on top, the sunlit parts are very white. |
| Cumulonimbus | 460–2,000 | Low dense cloud with tall tower shaped mass, often present in thunderstorms. |

# THE WORLD'S HIGH SPOTS

These are the highest points in the seven continents.

| Continent | Peak | Height |
|---|---|---|
| Africa | Mt. Kilimanjaro, Tanzania | 5,895 m |
| Antarctica | Vinson Massif | 5,140 m |
| Asia | Mt. Everest, Nepal-Tibet | 8,848 m |
| Australia | Mt. Kosciusko, New South Wales | 2,229 m |
| Europe | Mt. El'brus, USSR | 5,642 m |
| North America | Mt. McKinley, Alaska | 6,194 m |
| South America | Mt. Ojos del Salado, Chile-Argentina | 7,084 m |

# THE WORLD'S TOP TEN ACTIVE VOLCANOES

| Name | Range | Height (in metres) |
|---|---|---|
| Guallatiri | Andes | 6,060 |
| Lascar | Andes | 5,990 |
| Cotopaxi | Andes | 5,897 |
| Volcán Misti | Andes | 5,842 |
| Tupungatito | Andes | 5,640 |
| Popocatépetl | Altiplano de Mexico | 5,452 |
| Sangay | Andes | 5,230 |
| Cotacachi | Andes | 4,935 |
| Puracé | Andes | 4,756 |
| Klyuchevskaya | Sredinny Khrebet | 4,850 |

(The highest volcano in Europe is Mount Etna in Sicily, which is 3,363 m high.)

# Inventions

## MAJOR INVENTIONS AND SCIENTIFIC DISCOVERIES

| Achievement | Date | Inventor/Discoverer |
|---|---|---|
| Adding Machine | 1623 | Wilhelm Shickard (Germany) |
| Aeroplane | 1903 | Orville and Wilbur Wright (USA) |
| Air Conditioning | 1911 | Willis H. Carrier (USA) |
| Airship (non-rigid) | 1852 | Henri Giffard (France) |
| Arc Lamp | 1879 | C. F. Brush (USA) |
| Aspirin | 1893 | Hermann Dreser |

51

| Achievement | Date | Inventor/Discoverer |
|---|---|---|
| Bakelite | 1907 | Leo. H. Baekeland (Belgium/USA) |
| Balloon | 1783 | Jaques and Joseph Montgolfier (France) |
| Ball-Point Pen | 1888 | John Loud (USA) |
| Barbed Wire | 1867 | Lucien Smith |
| Barometer | 1643 | Evangelista Torricelli (Italy) |
| Bicycle | 1839 | Kirkpatrick Macmillan (Scotland) |

| Achievement | Date | Inventor/Discoverer |
|---|---|---|
| Bifocal Lens | 1780 | Benjamin Franklin (USA) |
| Bunsen Burner | 1855 | Robert von Bunsen (Germany) |
| Car (Internal Combustion) | 1860 | Jean Joseph Etienne Lenoir (France) |
| Car (Petrol driven) | 1886 | Karl-Friedrich Benz (Germany) |
| Carbon-dioxide and gases generally | 1848 | Johann Baptista van Helmont (Belgium) |
| Cash Register | 1879 | James Ritty (USA) |
| Cathode Ray Tube | 1897 | Karl Ferdinand Braun (Germany) |
| Celluloid | 1861 | Alexander Parkes (Britain) |
| Cement (Portland) | 1824 | Joseph Aspdin (Britain) |
| Chronometer | 1735 | John Harrison (Britain) |
| Clock (mechanical) | 725 | I-Hsing and Liang Ling-Tsan (China) |
| Clock (pendulum) | 1657 | Christian Huygens (Holland) |
| Combustion (theory of) | 1775 | Antoine Lavoisier (France) |
| DDT | 1939 | Paul Muller (Switzerland) |
| Dental Plate | 1817 | Anthony Plantson (USA) |
| Diesel Engine | 1895 | Rudolf Diesel (Germany) |
| Disc Brakes | 1902 | Dr. F. Lanchester (Britain) |
| Dyes (synthetic) | 1857 | William Perkins (Britain) |
| Dynamite | 1867 | Alfred Nobel (Sweden) |
| Dynamo | 1860 | Antonio Picinotti (Italy) |
| Electric Blanket | 1883 | Exhibited at Vienna Exhibition, Austria |
| Electric Generator (static) | 1660 | Otto von Guericke (Germany) |
| Electric Lamp | 1879 | Thomas Edison (USA) |
| Electric Motor (d.c.) | 1873 | Zenobe Gramme (Belgium) |
| (a.c.) | 1888 | Nikola Tesla (USA) |
| Electro magnet | 1824 | William Sturgeon (Britain) |
| Electrometer | 1788 | Alessandro Volta (Italy) |
| Electronic computer | 1942 | J. G. Brainerd, J. P. Eckert, J. W. Manchly (USA) |
| Film (moving) | 1885 | Louis le Prince |
| (musical sound) | 1923 | Dr. Lee de Forest (USA) |
| (talking) | 1926 | Warner Bros. (USA) |
| Fluorine | 1771 | Wilhelm Scheele (Sweden) |
| Fountain Pen | 1884 | Lewis Waterman (USA) |
| Gas Turbine Engine | 1791 | John Barber (Britain) |
| Gear (Differential) | 1828 | Onésiphore Pecquer (France) |

| Achievement | Date | Inventor/Discoverer |
|---|---|---|
| Glider | 1853 | Sir George Cayley (Britain) |
| Gramophone (phonograph) | 1878 | Thomas Edison (USA) |
| Gravity | 1682 | Isaac Newton (Britain) |
| Gyro Compass | 1911 | Elmer Sperry (USA) |
| Helicopter | 1924 | Etienne Ochmichen (Britain) |
| Hovercraft | 1955 | Sir Christopher Cockerell (Britain) |
| Hydrogen | 1766 | Henry Cavendish (Britain) |
| Incubator | 1666 | Cornelius Drebbel (Holland) |
| Jet Engine | 1929 | Sir Frank Whittle |
| Laser | 1960 | Dr. Charles Towney (USA) |
| Launderette | 1934 | J. F. Cantrell (USA) |
| Light (Wave theory of) | 1690 | Christian Huygens (Holland) |
| Lightning Conductor | 1752 | Benjamin Franklin (USA) |
| Linoleum | 1860 | Frederick Walton (Britain) |
| Locomotive | 1804 | Richard Trevithick (Britain) |
| Logarithms | 1614 | John Napier (Scotland) |
| Long-playing Record | 1948 | Dr. Peter Goldmark (USA) |
| Machine Gun | 1718 | James Puckle (Britain) |
| Magnetic Recording | 1898 | Vlademar Poulsen (Denmark) |
| Magnetism | 1600 | William Gilbert (Britain) |
| Margarine | 1863 | Hippolyte Mege-Mouries (France) |
| Match (safety) | 1855 | J. E. Lundstrom (Sweden) |
| Microphone | 1876 | Alexander Graham Bell (USA) |
| Microscope (electron) | 1939 | Vladimir Zworykin (Russia/USA) |
| Microscope | 1590 | Zacharias Jansen (Holland) |
| Morphine | 1805 | Friedrich Sertürner (Germany) |
| Motor Cycle | 1885 | Gottlieb Daimler (Germany) |
| Nitrogen | 1772 | Daniel Rutherford (Britain) |
| Nylon | 1937 | Wallace Carothers (USA) |
| Oxygen | 1774 | Joseph Priestley (Britain) Wilhelm Scheele (Sweden) |

| Achievement | Date | Inventor/Discoverer |
|---|---|---|
| Paper | 105 | China |
| Parachute | 1797 | Andre-Jacques Garnerin (France) |
| Parking Meter | 1935 | Carl C. Magee (USA) |
| Passenger Lift | 1852 | Elish G. Otis (USA) |
| Pendulum | 1602 | Galileo Galilei (Italy) |
| Piano | 1720 | Bartolommeo Cristofori (Italy) |
| Photography (on metal) | 1826 | J. Nicéphore Niépce (France) |
| Penicillin | 1940 | Alexander Fleming (Britain) |
| Radar | 1935 | Robert Watson-Watt (Britain) |
| Radio telegraphy | 1895 | Guglielmo Marconi (Italy) |
| Radium | 1898 | Pierre and Marie Curie (France) |
| Rare gases | 1894–8 | William Ramsey (Britain) |
| Rayon | 1883 | Joseph Swan (Britain) |
| Refrigerator | 1850 | James Harrison and Alexander Twining (USA) |
| Rubber (latex foam) | 1928 | E. A. Murphy (Britain) |
| Rubber (vulcanized) | 1841 | Charles Goodyear (USA) |
| Safety pin | 1849 | William Hunt (USA) |

| Safety Razor | 1847 | William Samuel Henson (Britain) |
|---|---|---|
| Silicones | 1904 | F. S. Kipping (Britain) |
| Slide Rule | 1621 | William Oughtred (Britain) |
| Sodium | 1807 | Humphrey Davy (Britain) |
| Sewing Machine | 1829 | Barthélemy Thimmonnier (France) |

| Achievement | Date | Inventor/Discoverer |
|---|---|---|
| Spectacles | 1289 | Venice |
| Steel production | 1855 | Henry Bessemer (Britain) |
| Tank | 1914 | Sir Ernest Swinton (Britain) |
| Telegraph | 1837 | William Coke, Charles Wheatstone (Britain) |
| Telephone | 1861 | Alexander Graham Bell (USA) J. Philip Reis (Germany) |
| Telescope | 1608 | Hans Lippershey (Holland) |
| Television | 1926 | John Logie Baird (Britain) |
| Terylene | 1941 | J. R. Whinfield, J. T. Dickson (Britain) |
| Thermometer | 1593 | Galileo Galilei (Italy) |
| Transistor | 1948 | Walter Brittain (USA) |
| Typewriter | 1829 | Austin Burt (USA) |
| Vitamins | 1930 | Frederick Hopkins (Britain) |
| Watch | 1462 | Bartholomew Manfredi (Italy) |
| Water Closet | 1589 | Sir John Harrington (Britain) |
| X-rays | 1895 | Wilhelm von Rontgen (Germany) |
| Zip Fastener | 1891 | Whitcomb L. Judson (USA) |

# January

January is the English name for the first month of the year. It comes from the Latin words 'Januarius mensis', which is the Latin name for the first month. Here are the Latin names for the twelve months of the year and their origins.

January – From Januarius, named after Janus the Roman God of doorways. He had two faces, one looking forwards, the other looking backwards, so that he could watch over the 'entrance' to the year.

February – From Februarius, a name which comes from 'Februa', a Roman festival of purification.

March – From Martius, which means 'of Mars'. Mars was the Roman God of war.

April – From Aprilis, which itself comes from the Latin verb 'aperire' which means 'to open out'. April is the month when flowers and blossom begin to open out.

May – From Maius, meaning 'of Maia'. Maia was a Roman goddess, the mother of Mercury.

June – From Junius, named after the goddess Juno, the wife of Jupiter.

July – From the name of the famous Roman general, Caius Julius Caesar, who was born in this month. The old name Quinctilis (the fifth month) was replaced by Julius after the dead general became a god.

August – From the name of the first Roman emperor, Augustus Caesar.

September – From September, which means 'of the seventh month'. 'Septem' is the Latin for 'seven'. The old Roman year originally began in March and only had ten months, so this was number seven.

October – Octo is the Latin for the number 'eight'. Like September, October refers to one of the months of the old Roman year, the eighth month.

November – The ninth month of the old Roman year was named after 'novem', the word for nine. November means 'of the ninth month'.

December – In Latin the number ten is 'decem', and December is named after the original tenth month, which was also the last month in the Roman year.


## 'JOVIS DIES' = THURSDAY – THE DAYS OF THE WEEK

'Jovis dies' was the Roman name for the fourth day of the week. The English name Thursday comes from the Old English equivalent of the Latin. Here is an explanation of the English names for all the days of the week.


## THE DAYS OF THE WEEK

The English names of the days of the week come from the Old English translations and equivalents of the Latin names of Roman Mythology.

| English | Latin | (translation) | Old English | (translation) |
|---|---|---|---|---|
| Sunday | dies solis | (day of the sun) | sunnandaeg | (day of the sun) |
| Monday | lunae dies | (day of the moon) | monandaeg | (day of the moon) |
| Tuesday | dies Martis | (day of Mars) | Tiwesdaeg | (day of Tiw) |
| Wednesday | Mercurii dies | (day of Mercury) | wodnesdaeg | (day of Woden) |
| Thursday | Jovis dies | (Jupiter's day) | thursdaeg | (day of Thor) |
| Friday | Veneris dies | (day of Venus) | frigedaeg | (day of Frig) |
| Saturday | Saturni dies | (day of Saturn) | Saeterdaeg | (day of Saturn) |

Tiw – The God of War in Old English was identified with Mars, the Roman God of War and Farming.

Woden – In Old English mythology, Woden was the god who granted victory in battle and the equivalent of Mercury the Roman messenger of Victory.

Thor – The Old English God of Thunder was the closest to Jupiter (or Jove), the chief of the Roman gods, because of the power they both possessed of controlling thunder and lightning.

Frig – The Old English Goddess of Love who was the equivalent of Venus, the Roman Goddess of Love.

Saturn – A planet named after an old god of Roman mythology who was responsible for agriculture and civilisation in general.

# Kings & Queens

## THE REIGNING MONARCHS OF THE WORLD

| Country | Title and Name |
|---------|----------------|
| Bahrain | His Highness Shaikh Isa ibn Sulman al-Khalifa |
| Belgium | His Majesty Baudoin Albert Charles Léopold Axel Marie Gustave, King of the Belgians |
| Bhutan | Jigme Singye Wangchuk, Druk Gyalpo (Dragon King) |

| | |
|---|---|
| Denmark | Her Majesty Queen Margrethe II |
| Japan | His Imperial Majesty Hirohito |
| Jordan | His Majesty King Husain ibn Talal |
| Kuwait | His Majesty Shaikh Jabir al-Ahmad al-Jabir as-Sabah, Amir |
| Lesotho | King Motlotlehi Moshoeshoe II |
| Liechtenstein | Prince Franz Josef II |
| Luxembourg | His Royal Highness Prince Jean Benoît Guillaume Marie Robert Louis Antoine Adolphe Marc d'Aviano |
| Malaysia | His Majesty Sultan Haji Ahmad Shah al Mustain Billah Ibri al-Marhuam Sultan Abu Bakar Ri-Ayatuddin al-Mu'adzah Shah (Sultan of Pahang) (Supreme Head of State) |
| Monaco | His Serene Highness Prince Rainier III |
| Morocco | His Majesty King Hassan II |
| Nepal | His Majesty King Birenda Bir Bikram Shah Dev |
| Netherlands | Her Majesty Queen Beatrix Wilhelmina Armgard |
| Norway | His Majesty King Olav V |
| Oman | Sultan Qaboos bin Said |
| Qatar | Shaikh Khalifa ibn Hamad al-Thani, Amir |
| Saudi Arabia | His Majesty King Khalid ibn Abdul-Aziz |
| Spain | His Majesty King Juan Carlos |
| Swaziland | His Majesty King Sobhuza II |
| Sweden | King Carl XVI Gustav |
| Thailand | His Majesty King Bhumibol Adulyadej |

| Tonga | His Majesty King Tauf'ahau Tupou IV |
| United Kingdom | Her Majesty Queen Elizabeth II (Elizabeth Alexandra Mary of Windsor) |
| Western Samoa | His Highness Malietoa Tanumafili II |

Life on the Ocean Wave

# LANDMARKS IN NAUTICAL HISTORY

| Date | | Event |
|---|---|---|
| B.C. | 7,250 | First evidence of sea traffic, in the Aegean. |
| | 330 | The Greek navigator Pytheas discovered the means of calculating latitude. |
| A.D. | c1280 | Compass in common use at sea. |
| | 1496 | First dry-dock completed at Portsmouth. |
| | 1508 | First Maritime Insurance in England. |
| | 1637 | Launching of the 'Royal Sovereign', first ship with 100 guns. |
| | 1748 | Uniforms instituted for officers. |
| | 1783 | First steam propelled vessel sailed in France. |
| | 1807 | World's first regular steamer service in operation on the east coast of the USA. |
| | 1825 | First steam voyage to India. |
| | 1827 | First crossing of the Atlantic by a power vessel, in 22 days. |
| | 1837 | Shells replaced Round Shot in Royal Naval guns. |
| | 1838 | First continuous crossing of the Atlantic by steam ship in 18 days 10 hours. |
| | 1838 | First screw propeller in use. |
| | 1857 | An international code of signals first founded. |
| | 1860 | 'Warrior', the first British ironclad, steam-powered battleship to go to sea. |
| | 1861 | First issue of gale warnings. |
| | 1863 | First use of twin screw propellers. |
| | 1869 | Opening of the Suez Canal. |
| | 1881 | Principle of breech-loading adopted by the Admiralty. |
| | 1894 | Building of the first turbine-powered ship the 'Turbinia'. |

| 1900 | Admiralty adopted Wireless Telegraphy. |
| 1901 | Launching of the first British submarine. |
| 1907 | Launching of the first British battle cruiser. |
| 1912 | Sinking of the 'Titanic', the largest steamship afloat, with the loss of 1,513 lives. |
| 1934 | Launching of the 'Queen Mary'. |
| 1945 | Torpedoing of the German liner 'Willem Gustloff' caused the greatest loss of life from any single ship-wreck, an estimated 7,700. |
| 1958 | First passage by a nuclear submarine under the North Pole. |
| 1959 | Official opening of the St Lawrence Seaway. |
| 1967 | HMS 'Valiant' completed a 12,000 mile (19,310 km) submerged voyage from Singapore to Clyde in 27 days. |
| 1968 | First Polaris missile fired from a British nuclear submarine HMS 'Resolution'. |
| 1970 | Last issue of rum in the Royal Navy. |
| 1972 | The Royal Navy's first plastic warship HMS Wilton brought into operation. |
| 1976 | The oil tanker 'Olympic Bravery' ran aground off the French coast on her maiden voyage, so becoming the largest shipwreck in history. |

## NAUTICAL EXPRESSIONS

| abaft | behind |
| aft | towards the stern (rear of the ship) |
| avast | stop, hold fast |
| awash | to be level with the surface of the water |
| ballast | weight placed in a ship to keep her stable |

| | |
|---|---|
| beakhead | part of a ship in front of the forecastle |
| belay | to secure a rope to a fixed object (cleat or bollard) |
| bilge | the broadest part of a ship's bottom on which she would rest if aground |
| binnacle | the compass housing case |
| bulkhead | an upright partition which divides the hold or cabins |
| by the head | to be deeper in the water forward than aft |
| companion | hatch covering made of wood |
| check | to let a rope out a little. To stop progress |
| deadlight | shutter for protecting a cabin window in a storm |
| displacement | the amount of water displaced by a vessel afloat |
| draught | the depth to which the lowest part of a ship sinks below the waterline |
| ebb | the return of the tide-water towards the sea |
| flood | the rise of the tide and the opposite to the ebb |
| fluke | the part of the anchor that catches the sea bed |
| fore-and-aft | in a direction from bow to stern |
| forecastle | a short raised deck in front part of a ship – the forepart of a ship where the crew lives |
| galley | the ship's kitchen |
| halyard | a rope or tackle used for raising a sail or a flag |
| hawser | a small cable |
| land fall | the first sighting of land while at sea |
| lee | the sheltered side of a ship. |
| neap tides | tides which rise and fall the least |
| poop | the aftermost part of ship |
| port | the left side of the ship looking towards the bows |

| | |
|---|---|
| ratlings | rope steps laced horizontally across the shrouds to form a ladder |
| scuppers | drain holes in sides of ship |
| shrouds | the wire ropes which extend from the head of a mast to both sides of the ship and support the mast upright |
| stay | a rope supporting a mast |
| superstructure | the parts of a ship built above the upper deck |
| trim | the appearance of a ship as she floats |
| truck | the circular mast-head cap |
| weather side | the side of the ship against which the wind is blowing, the opposite of the lee |
| weather tide | a tide which carries a ship windward |
| weigh | to draw up the anchor |
| yaw | the movement of a ship's head from side to side caused by poor steering or the condition of the sea |

## SHIP'S TIME

| | |
|---|---|
| Forenoon Watch | 8 am to Noon |
| Afternoon Watch | Noon to 4 pm |
| Dog Watches | 4 pm to 6 pm |
| | 6 pm to 8 pm |
| First Watch | 8 pm to Midnight |
| Middle Watch | Midnight to 4 pm |
| Morning Watch | 4 am to 8 am |

Except for the Dog Watches, time is kept during each watch by a bell being struck every half-hour, with one bell at the first half hour through to eight bells at the fourth hour. In the Dog Watches one bell is struck at 6.30 pm, two bells at 7 pm, three bells at 7.30 pm and eight bells at 8 pm, this is because the Dog Watches are shorter than the other five in order that the same crew do not have the same hours for duty each day.

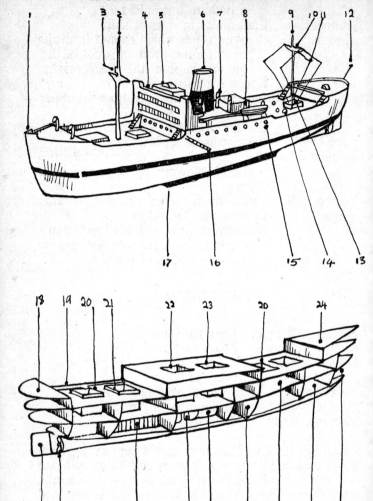

1. Jackstaff. 2. Foremast. 3. Crow's-nest. 4. Navigating bridge. 5. Wheelhouse. 6. Funnel. 7. Cowl ventilators. 8. Life-boat and davits. 9. Mainmast. 10. Cross-tree. 11. Derrick. 12. Ensign staff. 13. Cargo hatch. 14. Winch. 15. Porthole. 16. Accommodation ladder. 17. Bilge keel. 18. Poop. 19. Bulwark. 20. Well-deck. 21. Hatch coaming. 22. Engine casing to skylight. 23. Boiler casing to funnel. 24. Forecastle. 25. Forepeak. 26. Cargo hold. 27. 'Tween-decks. 28. Watertight bulkhead. 29. Boiler-room or stokehold. 30. Engine-room. 31. Shaft tunnel. 32. Propeller or screw. 33. Rudder.

# TEN OF THE WORLD'S FASTEST VOYAGES

| Date | Voyage | Mariners | Duration |
|------|--------|----------|----------|
| 1905 | Sailing across the Atlantic in a monohull yacht | W. Marshall and crew (USA) | 12 days 4 hr. |
| 1916 | Sailing across the Atlantic in a sailing ship | Captain and crew of the 'Lancing' (USA) | 6 days 18 hr. |
| 1922 | Solo sailing across the Atlantic (West–East) | J. V. T. Macdonald (GB) | 16 days |
| 1934 | Solo sailing across the Atlantic (East–West) | R. D. Graham (GB) | 24.35 days |
| 1968 | Sailing across the Atlantic in a multihull yacht | E. Tabarly (France) and 2 crew | 10 days 12 hr. |
| 1970 | Solo rowing across the Atlantic (East to West) | S. Genders (GB) | 162 days 18 hr. |
| 1973–74 | Solo sailing round the world | A. Colas (France) | 167 days |
| 1973–74 | Solo sailing round the world (westabout) | K. Horie (Japan) | 275 days 13 hr. |
| 1976 | Solo sailing across the Atlantic by a woman | C. Francis (GB) | 29 days 1 hr. 52 mins. |
| 1977 | Sailing across the Pacific | W. Lee (USA) | 8 days 11 hr. 1 min. |

## THE WORLD'S MONEY

| | |
|---|---|
| Afghanistan | Afghani of 100 Puls |
| Albania | Lek of 100 Quindarka |
| Algeria | Dinar of 100 Centimes |
| Andorra | French Franc and Spanish Peseta |
| Angola | Kwanza of 100 Lweis |
| Antigua | East Caribbean Dollar of 100 Cents |
| Argentina | Peso of 100 Centavos |
| Australia | Dollar of 100 Cents |
| Austria | Schilling of 100 Groschen |

| | |
|---|---|
| Bahamas | Bahemian Dollar of 100 Cents |
| Bahrain | Dinar of 1,000 Fils |
| Bangladesh | Bangladesh Taka of 100 Paise |
| Barbados | Dollar of 100 Cents |
| Belgium | Belgian Franc of 100 Centimes |
| Belize | Belizean Dollar of 100 Cents |
| Benin | CFA Franc of 100 Centimes |
| Bhutan | Ngultrum of 100 Paisa |
| Bolivia | Peso of 100 Centavos |
| Botswana | S.A. Rand of 100 Cents |
| Brazil | Cruzeiro of 100 Centavos |
| Brunei | Brunei Dollar of 100 Sen |
| Bulgaria | Lev of 100 Stotinki |
| Burma | Kyat of 100 Pyas |
| Burundi | Burundi Franc |
| Cameroon (Federal Republic of) | Franc C.F.A. of 100 Centimes |
| Canada | Dollar of 100 Cents |
| Cape Verde Islands | Escudo of 100 Centavos |
| Cayman Islands | Dollar of 100 Cents |
| Central African Empire | Franc C.F.A. of 100 Centimes |
| Chad | Franc C.F.A. of 100 Centimes |
| Chile | Escudo of 100 Centésimos |
| China | Renminbi or Yuan of 10 Jiao or 100 Fen |
| Christmas Island | Australian Dollar of 100 Cents |
| Comoro Islands | Franc C.F.A. of 100 Centimes |
| Colombia | Peso of 100 Centavos |
| Congo | Franc C.F.A. of 100 Centimes |
| Costa Rica | Colon of 100 Céntimos |
| Cuba | Peso of 100 Centavos |
| Cyprus | Cyprus Pound of 1,000 Mils |
| Czechoslovakia | Koruna of 100 Haléru |
| Dahomey (Republic of) | Franc C.F.A. of 100 Centimes |
| Denmark | Krone of 100 øre |
| Djibouti | Djibouti Franc of 100 Centimes |
| Dominican Republic | Peso of 100 Centavos |
| East Caribbean Territory | East Caribbean Dollar of 100 Cents |
| Ecuador | Sucre of 100 Centavos |
| Egypt | Egyptian Pound of 100 Piastres or 1,000 Millièmes |
| El Salvador | Colon of 100 Centavos |
| Equatorial Guinea | Ekpwele of 100 Centimes |
| Ethiopia | Ethiopian Dollar of 100 Cents |
| Falkland Islands | Pound of 100 pence |
| Faröe Islands | Krone of 100 øre |
| Fiji | Fiji Dollar of 100 Cents |
| Finland | Markka of 100 Penniä |

| | |
|---|---|
| France | Franc of 100 Centimes |
| French Community (Republics of Gabon, Congo, Central Africa and Chad) | Franc C.F.A. of 100 Centimes |
| French Guiana | Franc of 100 Centimes |
| French Polynesia | Franc C.F.A. of 100 Centimes |
| Gambia | Dalasi of 100 Bututs |
| Germany (East) | Mark der Deutschen Demokratischen Republik (M) of 100 Pfennig |
| Germany (Federal Republic of) | Deutsche Mark of 100 Pfennig |
| Ghana | Cedi of 100 Pesewa |
| Gibraltar | Pound of 100 Pence |
| Gilbert Islands | Australian Dollar of 100 Cents |
| Greece | Drachma of 100 Lepta |
| Greenland | Danish Krone of 100 øre |
| Guadeloupe | Franc of 100 Centimes |
| Guatemala | Quetzal of 100 Centavos |
| Guinea (Republic of) | Sily of 100 Corilles |
| Guinea Bissau | Guinea Bissau Escudo of 100 Centavos |
| Guyana | Guyana Dollar of 100 Cents |
| Haiti | Gourde of 100 Centimes |
| Honduras | Lempira of 100 Centavos |
| Hong Kong | Hong Kong Dollar of 100 Cents |
| Hungary | Forint of 100 Fillér |
| Iceland | Krona of 100 Aurar |
| India | Rupee of 100 Paise |
| Indonesia | Rupiah of 100 Sen |
| Iran | Rial of 100 Dinars |
| Iraq | Iraqi Dinar of 1,000 Fils |
| Ireland (Republic of) | Pound of 100 Pence |
| Israel | Israel Pound of 100 Agorot |
| Italy | Lira |
| Ivory Coast (Republic of) | Franc C.F.A. of 100 Centimes |
| Jamaica | Jamaican Dollar of 100 Cents |
| Japan | Yen of 100 Sen |
| Johnston Island | US Dollar of 100 Cents |
| Jordan (Hashemite Kingdom of) | Jordanian Dinar of 1,000 Fils |
| Kampuchea | Riel of 100 Sen |
| Kenya | Kenya Schilling of 100 Cents |
| Korea (North) | Won of 100 Jeon |
| Korea, Republic of South Korea | Won of 100 Jeon |
| Kuwait | Kuwait Dinar of 1,000 Fils |
| Laos | Kip of 100 Ats |

| | |
|---|---|
| Lebanon | Lebanese Pound of 100 Piastres |
| Liberia | Liberian Dollar of 100 Cents |
| Libya | Libyan Dinar of 1,000 Dirhams |
| Liechtenstein | Swiss Franc of 100 Centimes |
| Luxembourg | Franc of 100 Centimes |
| Macao | Pataca of 100 Avos |
| Madagascar | Madagascar Franc of 100 Centimes |
| Malawi | Malawi Kwacha of 100 Tambala |
| Malaysia | Malaysian Dollar (Ringit) of 100 Cents |
| Mali (Republic of) | Franc Mali of 100 Centimes |
| Maldives | Maldivian Rupee of 100 Laris |
| Malta | Maltese Pound of 100 Cents or 1,000 Mils |
| Martinique | Franc of 100 Centimes |
| Mauretania | Ouguiya of 5 khoums |
| Mauritius | Rupee of 100 Cents |
| Mexico | Peso of 100 Centavos |
| Mongolia | Tugrik of 100 Mongo |
| Morocco | Dirham of 100 Centimes |
| Mozambique | Escudo of 100 Centavos |
| Namibia | S.A. Rand of 100 Cents |

| | |
|---|---|
| Nauru | Australian Dollar of 100 Cents |
| Nepal | Rupee of 100 Paisa |
| Netherlands (The) | Florin (Guilder) of 100 Cents |
| Netherlands Antilles (The) | N.A. Guilder of 100 Cents |
| New Caledonia | Franc CFP of 100 Centimes |
| New Hebrides | New Hebridean Franc of 100 Centimes |
| New Zealand | New Zealand Dollar of 100 Cents |
| Nicaragua | Córdoba of 100 Centavos |
| Niger (Republic of) | Franc C.F.A. of 100 Centimes |
| Nigeria (Federal Republic of) | Naira of 100 Kobo |
| Niue | New Zealand Dollar of 100 Cents |
| Norfolk Island | Australian Dollar of 100 Cents |
| Norway | Krone of 100 øre |
| Oman | Rial Omani of 1,000 Baiza |
| Pakistan | Rupee of 100 Paisa |
| Panama | Balboa of 100 Cents |
| Papua New Guinea | Kina of 100 Toea |
| Paraguay | Guarani of 100 Céntimos |
| Peru | Gold Sol of 100 Centavos |
| Philippines | Philippine Peso of 100 Centavos |
| Pitcairn Island | New Zealand Dollar of 100 Cents |
| Poland | Zloty of 100 Groszy |

| | |
|---|---|
| Portugal | Escudo of 100 Centavos |
| Qatar | Qatar Riyal of 100 Dirhams |
| Reunion | Franc C.F.A. of 100 Centimes |
| Rhodesia | Dollar of 100 Cents |
| Rumania | Leu of 100 Bani |
| Rwanda | Rwanda Franc of 100 Centimes |
| Sahara, Western | Spanish Peseta of 100 Céntimos |
| Saint Helena | UK Pound of 100 Pence |
| Samoa (Western) | Tala of 100 Sene |
| St. Tomé and Principé | Escudo of 100 Centavos |
| Saudi Arabia | Riyal of 20 Qursh or 100 Halalas |
| Senegal | Franc.C.F.A. of 100 Centimes |
| Seychelles | Rupee of 100 Cents |
| Sierra Leone | Leone of 100 Cents |
| Singapore | S. Dollar of 100 Cents |
| Somalia | Somali Shilling of 100 Cents |
| South Africa | Rand of 100 Cents |
| Spain | Peseta of 100 Céntimos |
| Sri Lanka | Rupee of 100 Cents |
| Sudan | Sudanese Pound of 100 Piastres or 1,000 Milliemes |
| Surinam | Guilder of 100 Cents |
| Swaziland | Lilangeni of 100 Cents |
| Sweden | Krona of 100 öre |
| Switzerland | Franc of 100 Centimes |
| St. Pierre and Miquelon | Franc of 100 Centimes |
| Syria | Syrian Pound of 100 Piastres |
| Taiwan | Taiwan Dollar of 100 Cents |
| Tanzania | T. Shilling of 100 Cents |
| Thailand | Baht of 100 Stangs |
| Timor East | Timor Escudo of 100 Centavos |
| Togo (Republic of) | Franc C.F.A. of 100 Centimes |
| Tonga | Pa'anga of 100 Seniti |
| Trinidad and Tobago | Trinidad and Tobago Dollar of 100 Cents |
| Tunisia | Tunisian Dinar of 1,000 Millimes |
| Turkey | Turkish Lira of 100 Kurus |
| Tuvalu | Australian Dollar of 100 Cents |
| Uganda | U. Shilling of 100 Cents |
| United Arab Emirates | Dirham of 100 Fils |
| United Kingdom | Pound of 100 new pence |
| United States of America | Dollar of 100 Cents |
| Upper Volta (Republic of) | Franc C.F.A. of 100 Centimes |
| Uruguay | Peso of 100 Centésimos |
| U.S.S.R. | Rouble of 100 Copecks |
| Venezuela | Bolívar of 100 Céntimos |

| | |
|---|---|
| Vietnam | Dong of 10 Hào or 100 Xu |
| Wake Island | US Dollar of 100 Cents |
| Wall Is. and Futuna Islands | Franc C.F.P. of 100 Centimes |
| Yemen (Arab Republic) | Riyal of 100 Fils |
| Yemen (People's Democratic Republic) | Southern Yemen Dinar (YD) of 1,000 Fils |
| Yugoslavia | Dinar of 100 Paras |
| Zaire | Zaire of 100 Makuta or 10,000 Sengi |
| Zambia | Kwacha of 100 Ngwee |

Numerals &+

The numerals which we use today came originally from Arabic numerals. However, there are many different types of numerals which have been used throughout history, and these are some of them:

## ARABIC NUMERALS

七 7
八 8
九 9
十 10
百 100
千 1000
萬 10000

一 1
二 2
三 3
四 4
五 5
六 6

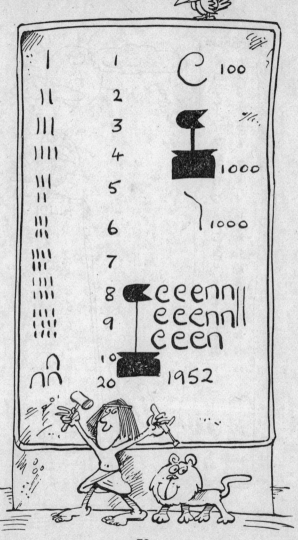

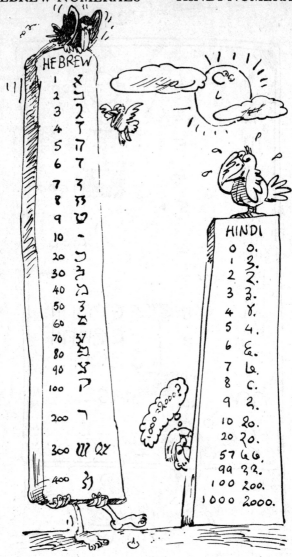

# ROMAN NUMERALS

| | | | |
|---|---|---|---|
| I. . . 1 | | XI. . . 11 | |
| II. . . 2 | | XII. . . 12 | |
| III. . . 3 | | XIII. . . 13 | |
| IV. . . 4 | | XIV. . . 14 | |
| V. . . 5 | | XV. . . 15 | |
| VI. . . 6 | | XVI. . . 16 | |
| VII. . . 7 | | XVII. . . 17 | |
| VIII. . . 8 | | XVIII. . . 18 | |
| IX. . . 9 | | XIX. . . 19 | |
| X. . . 10 | | XX. . . 20 | |
| | | | |
| XXX. . . 30 | | LXX. . . 70 | |
| XL. . . 40 | | LXXX. . . 80 | |
| L. . . 50 | | XC. . . 90 | |
| LX. . . 60 | | C. . . 100 | |
| | | | |
| CCC. . . 300 | | M. . . 1000 | |
| CD. . . 400 | | MD. . . 1500 | |
| D. . . 500 | | MCMLII. . . 1952 | |
| CM. . . 900 | | MM. . . 2000 | |

Outer Space

# THE SUN

| | |
|---|---|
| Age | At least 6,000 million years old |
| Diameter | 1,391,980 km |
| Surface Area | 12,000 times that of Earth |
| Temperature | Surface:  About 6,000°C |
| | Internal:  About 35,000,000°C |
| Distance from the Earth | 149,597,906 km |

# THE MOON

| | |
|---|---|
| Diameter | 3,475.6 km |
| Surface Area | 37,969,400 km² |
| Temperature | |
| (on lunar equator) | Day: estimated + 220°F |
| | Night: estimated −250°F |
| Distance from the Earth | Maximum: 406,697 km |
| | Minimum: 356,410 km |

# THE PLANETS

| Planet | Distance from the Earth Maximum (in km) | Minimum (in km) | Distance from the sun (in km) | Period of revolution round the sun |
|---|---|---|---|---|
| Mercury | 220,317,000 | 79,000,000 | 57,900,000 | 88 days |
| Venus | 259,000,000 | 39,750,000 | 108,200,000 | 224.7 days |
| Earth | – | – | 149,600,000 | 365.3 days |
| Mars | 397,500,000 | 55,000,000 | 227,900,000 | 687 days |
| Jupiter | 960,700,000 | 582,600,000 | 778,300,000 | 11.9 years |
| Saturn | 1,646,000,000 | 1,244,000,000 | 1,427,000,000 | 29.5 years |
| Uranus | 1,946,000,000 | 1,594,000,000 | 1,783,000,000 | 84 years |
| Neptune | 2,891,000,000 | 2,654,000,000 | 2,793,000,000 | 164.8 years |
| Pluto | 4,506,000,000 | 2,605,000,000 | 3,666,000,000 | 248.4 years |

# THE CONSTELLATIONS

These are the most important constellations – or groups of stars – in the northern hemisphere.

| Scientific Name | English Name |
|---|---|
| Andromeda | The Chained Lady |
| Auriga | The Charioteer |
| Bootes | The Herdsman |
| Canis Major | The Greater Dog |
| Canis Minor | The Smaller Dog |
| Cassiopeia | The wife of Cephus |
| Cygnus | The Swan |
| Gemini | The Twins |
| Leo | The Lion |
| Lyra | The Lyre or Harp |
| Pegasus | The Winged Horse |
| Perseus | The Legendary Hero |
| Sagittarius | The Archer |
| Scorpius | The Scorpion |
| Taurus | The Bull |
| Ursa Major | The Great Bear |
| Ursa Minor | The Little Bear |

# MAN IN SPACE – WHO, WHEN AND FOR HOW LONG

| Date | Pilot | Country | Spacecraft | Flight Duration days | hrs. | mins. |
|---|---|---|---|---|---|---|
| 1961 | | | | | | |
| April 12th | Yuri Gagarin (aged 27) (First man in space) | USSR | Vostok 1 | | 1 | 48 |
| May 5th | Alan Shepard (37) (First American in space) | USA | Freedom 7 | | | 15 |

| Date | Pilot | Country | Spacecraft | Flight Duration days | hrs. | mins. |
|------|-------|---------|------------|------|------|-------|
| July 21st | Virgil Grissom (34) | USA | Liberty Bell 7 | | | 16 |
| Aug 6–7th | Gherman Stepanovich Titov (26) | USSR | Vostok 2 | 1 | 1 | 18 |
| *1962* Feb 20th | John Glenn (40) (First American manned space-craft to enter Earth orbit) | USA | Friendship | | 4 | 55 |
| May 24th | Malcolm Carpenter (37) | USA | Aurora 7 | | 4 | 56 |
| Aug 11–15th | Andrian Nikolayev (32) (first man-operated television from space) | USSR | Vostok 3 | 3 | 22 | 22 |
| Aug 12–15th | Pavel Popovich (31) | USSR | Vostok 4 | 2 | 22 | 57 |

| Date | Pilot | Country | Spacecraft | Flight Duration | | |
|------|-------|---------|-----------|------|------|------|
| | | | | days | hrs. | mins. |
| Oct | Walter Schirra (39) | USA | Sigma 7 | | 9 | 13 |
| *1963* May 15–16th | Leroy Cooper (36) (Manual re-entry after failure of automatic control system) | USA | Faith 7 | 1 | 10 | 20 |
| June 14–19th | Valeriy Bykovsky (28) | USSR | Vostok 5 | 4 | 23 | 66 |
| June 16–19th | Valentina Tereshkova (26) (First woman in space) | USSR | Vostok 6 | 3 | 22 | 50 |
| *1964* Oct 12–13th | Vladimir Komarov (37) Boris Yegorov (37) Konstantin Feoktiskov (38) | USSR | Voskhod 1 | 1 | 0 | 17 |
| *1965* March 18–19th | Alexei Leonov (30) Pavel Belyavev (39) (Leonov became the first man to float in outer space) | USSR | Voskhod 2 | 1 | 2 | 2 |
| March 23rd | Virgil Grissom (38) John Young | USA | Gemini 3 | | 4 | 53 |
| June 3–7th | James McDivitt (35) Edward White (34) (White took first space walk by an American) | USA | Gemini 4 | 4 | 1 | 56 |

| Date | Pilot | Country | Spacecraft | Flight Duration | | |
|------|-------|---------|------------|------|------|------|
| | | | | days | hrs. | mins. |
| Aug 21–29th | Leroy Cooper (38) Charles Conrad (35) | USA | Gemini 5 | 7 | 22 | 56 |
| Dec 4–18th | Frank Borman (37) James Lovell (37) (rendezvous with Gemini 6) | USA | Gemini 7 | 13 | 18 | 35 |
| Dec 15–16th | Walter Marty Shirra (43) Thomas Stafford (35) | USA | Gemini 6 | 1 | 1 | 51 |
| *1966* March 16th | Neil Armstrong (36) David Scott (36) (First docking between manned and unmanned spacecraft – Agena 7) | USA | Gemini 8 | | 10 | 42 |
| June 3–6th | Thomas Stafford (36) Eugene Cernan (32) (Longest space walk to date – 129 minutes by Cernan) | USA | Gemini 9 | 3 | 0 | 21 |
| July 18–25th | John Young; Michael Collins (space walk by Collins) | USA | Gemini 10 | 2 | 23 | 14 |
| Sept 12–15th | Charles Conrad (36); Richard Gordon (space walk by Gordon) | USA | Gemini 11 | 2 | 23 | 17 |

| Date | Pilot | Country | Spacecraft | Flight Duration | | |
|------|-------|---------|------------|-------|------|-------|
| | | | | days | hrs. | mins. |
| Nov 11–15th | James Lovell (38); Edwin Aldrin (36) (Docking with an Agena vehicle. Space walks by Aldrin totalling 5½ hours) | USA | Gemini 12 | 3 | 22 | 35 |
| *1967* April 22–23rd | Vladimir Komarov (40) (killed when his landing parachute tangled) | USSR | Soyuz 1 | 1 | 2 | 45 |
| Oct 11–22nd | Walter Shirra (45); Don Eisele (38); Walter Cunningham (36) (first flight of capsule designed ultimately for 7-day voyage to the Moon) | USA | Apollo VII | 10 | 20 | 9 |
| Oct 26–30th | Georgiy Beregovoiy (47) (Rendezvous with unmanned Soyuz 2) | USSR | Soyuz 3 | 3 | 22 | 51 |
| Dec 21–27th | Frank Borman (40); James Lovell (40); William Anders (35) (First men to break free from the Earth's gravitational field. First men to orbit the Moon. Christmas radio greetings sent from astronauts while in Moon orbit) | USA | Apollo VIII | 6 | 3 | 0 |

| Date | Pilot | Country | Spacecraft | Flight Duration | | |
|------|-------|---------|------------|------|------|------|
| | | | | days | hrs. | mins. |

*1969*

| Date | Pilot | Country | Spacecraft | days | hrs. | mins. |
|------|-------|---------|------------|------|------|------|
| Jan 14–17th | Vladimir Shatalov (41); Alexei Yeliseyev (34); Yevgeny Khrunov (35) | USSR | Soyuz 4 | 3 | 23 | 14 |
| Jan 15–18th | Boris Volynov (34) (Docked with Soyuz 4. First joining of two manned spacecraft in orbit. Yeliseyev and Khrunov transferred to – and landed in – Soyuz 5) | USSR | Soyuz 5 | 3 | 0 | 46 |
| March 3–13th | James McDivitt (39); David Scott (36); Russell Schweikart (33) (First trial of module-manned in space. Crew transferred through interior connection) | USA | Apollo IX | 10 | 1 | 1 |
| May 18–26th | Thomas Stafford (38); Eugene Cernan (35); John Young (38) | USA | Apollo X | 8 | 0 | 3 |
| July 16–24th | Neil Armstrong (38); Edwin Aldrin (39); Michael Collins (First Moon landing by man – Armstrong. Moon rock brought back to Earth) | USA | Apollo XI | 8 | 3 | 18 |

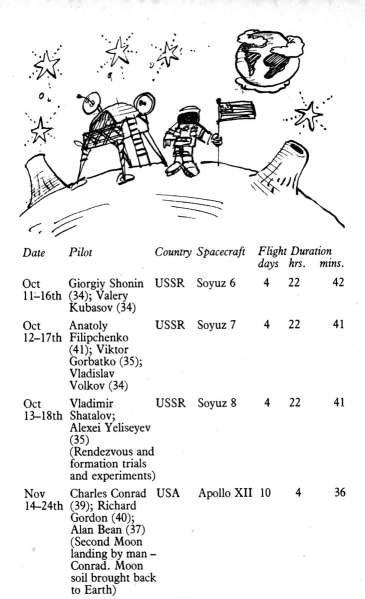

| Date | Pilot | Country | Spacecraft | Flight Duration | | |
|------|-------|---------|------------|------|------|------|
| | | | | days | hrs. | mins. |
| Oct 11–16th | Giorgiy Shonin (34); Valery Kubasov (34) | USSR | Soyuz 6 | 4 | 22 | 42 |
| Oct 12–17th | Anatoly Filipchenko (41); Viktor Gorbatko (35); Vladislav Volkov (34) | USSR | Soyuz 7 | 4 | 22 | 41 |
| Oct 13–18th | Vladimir Shatalov; Alexei Yeliseyev (35) (Rendezvous and formation trials and experiments) | USSR | Soyuz 8 | 4 | 22 | 41 |
| Nov 14–24th | Charles Conrad (39); Richard Gordon (40); Alan Bean (37) (Second Moon landing by man – Conrad. Moon soil brought back to Earth) | USA | Apollo XII | 10 | 4 | 36 |

90

| Date | Pilot | Country | Spacecraft | Flight Duration days | hrs. | mins. |
|------|-------|---------|------------|------|------|------|
| *1970* | | | | | | |
| April 11th | James Lovell (42); Fred Haise (36); John Sigert (38); (Landing on Moon abandoned after explosion in service module of spacecraft) | USA | Apollo XIII | 5 | 22 | 54 |
| June 1st | Andrian Nikolayev (33); Vitaly Sevastoyanov (35) | USSR | Soyuz 9 | 17 | 17 | 0 |
| *1971* Jan 31st | Alan Shepard (47); Edgar Mitchell (40); Stuart Roosa (37) | USA | Apollo XIV | 9 | 0 | 2 |
| April 23rd | Vladimir Shatalov (43); Alexei Yeliseyev (36); Nikolai Rukavishnikov (39) | USSR | Soyuz 10 | 1 | 23 | 45 |
| June 6th | George Dobrovolsky (43); Vladislav Volkov (35); Viktor Patsayev (37) (Spent 24 days in space but when spacecraft returned to Earth the three cosmonauts were found dead in their seats) | USSR | Soyuz 11 | 24 | | |
| July 26th | David Scott (39); Alfred Worden (39); James Irwin (41) | USA | Apollo XV | 12 | 7 | 12 |

| Date | Pilot | Country | Spacecraft | Flight Duration | | |
|------|-------|---------|-----------|------|------|------|
| | | | | days | hrs. | mins. |
| *1972* | | | | | | |
| April 16th | John Young (41); Charles Duke (36); Thomas Mattingley (36) | USA | Apollo XVI | 11 | 1 | 51 |
| Dec 7th | Harrison Schmitt (37); Eugene Cernan (39); Ronald Evans (Collected red and orange rock: left complex package of instruments on Moon which continue to send back messages) | USA | Apollo XVII | 12 | 16 | 32 |
| *1973* | | | | | | |
| Sept 27th | Vasili Lasarev (45); Oleg Makarov (40) | USSR | Soyuz 12 | 2 | | |
| Dec 18th | Pyotr Killimuk (31); Valentin Lebedev (31) | USSR | Soyuz 13 | 8 | | |
| *1974* | | | | | | |
| July 3rd | Pavel Popovich (44); Zyiri Artyukhin (44) | USSR | Soyuz 14 | 16 | | |
| Aug 27th | Gennady Sarafanov (32); Lev Demlin (48) | USSR | Soyuz 15 | 2 | | |
| Dec 2nd | Anatoly Filipchenko (47); Nikolai Rukavishnikov (41) ASTP (Apollo/Soyuz Test Project) flight test | USSR | Soyuz 16 | 6 | | 4 |

| Date | Pilot | Country | Spacecraft | Flight Duration | | |
|------|-------|---------|-----------|------|------|-------|
| | | | | days | hrs. | mins. |
| *1975*<br>Jan<br>11th | Alexei<br>Gubarev (43);<br>Georgy Grecho<br>(43) (Docked<br>with Salyut 4 for<br>677 hr. 8 min.) | USSR | Soyuz 17 | 29 | | 20 |
| April<br>5th | Vasily Lazarev;<br>Oleg Makarov<br>(Flight failure) | USSR | Soyuz<br>'anomaly' | | Sub-orbital | |
| May<br>24th | Pyotr Klimuk;<br>Vitaly<br>Sevastyanov<br>(Docked with<br>Salyut 4) | USSR | Soyuz 18 | 62 | 23 | 20 |
| July<br>15th | Alexei Leonov;<br>Valery Kubasov<br>(ASTP mission<br>docked with<br>Apollo 18 for<br>about 2 days) | USSR | Soyuz 19 | 5 | 22 | 31 |
| July<br>15th | Thomas Stafford;<br>Vance Brand;<br>Donald Slayton<br>(Docked with<br>Soyuz 19 for<br>crew exchanges<br>and joint<br>experiments) | USA | Apollo 18<br>ASTP | 9 | 1 | 28 |
| *1976*<br>July<br>6th | Boris Volynov;<br>Vitaly Zhdobov<br>(Docked with<br>Salyut 5 for<br>scientific<br>experiments) | USSR | Soyuz 21 | 49 | 6 | 24 |
| Sept<br>15th | Valery Bykovsky;<br>Vladimir<br>Aksyonov<br>(Photographic<br>mission with East<br>German cameras) | USSR | Soyuz 22 | 7 | 21 | 54 |

| Date | Pilot | Country | Spacecraft | Flight Duration | | |
|------|-------|---------|-----------|------|------|------|
| | | | | days | hrs. | mins. |
| 1976 Oct 14th | Vyacheslav Zudov; Valery Rozhdestvensky (Failed to dock with Salyut 5 due to faulty automatic control system) | USSR | Soyuz 23 | 2 | 0 | 6 |
| 1977 Feb 7th | Viktor Gorbatko; Yuri Glaskov (Docked with Salyut 5 for scientific research) | USSR | Soyuz 24 | 18 | | |
| Oct 9–11th | Vladimir Kovalenok; Valery Ryumin (Failed to dock with Salyut 6) | USSR | Soyuz 25 | 2 | | |
| Dec 10th – March 16th | Yuri Romanenko; Georgi Grechko (docked with Salyut 6 for scientific research, also performed in-space refuelling on Progress I) | USSR | Soyuz 26 | 96 | | |
| 1978 Jan 10–16th | Vladimir Dzhamibekov; Oleg Makarov (First simultaneous docking in space, all four astronauts met in the space lab together) | USSR | Soyuz 27 | 5 | | |

| Date | Pilot | Country | Spacecraft | Flight Duration | | |
|------|-------|---------|------------|------|------|------|
| | | | | days | hrs. | mins. |
| 1978 March 3–10th | Alexei Gubarev; Vladimir Remek (Czech) (First non-American, non-Russian in space. Rendezvous with Soyuz 26) | USSR | Soyuz 28 | 8 | | |
| June 15th | Vladimir Kovalenok; Alexander Ivanchenkov (Attempt in space thereby to break record 96 days in space. Docked with Salyut 6 for scientific work) | USSR | Soyuz 29 | (September 17 passed record of 96 days 10 hours creating a new record) | | |
| June 27– July 5 | Pyotr Klimuk; Miroslav Hermaszewski (Polish) (First Pole in space; flew on a supply mission to Salyut 6) | USSR | Soyuz 30 | 9 | | |

## PRE-CAMBRIAN TO THE PRESENT – THE DEVELOPMENT OF LIFE

The Pre-Cambrian era is the name given to the very earliest stage of world development, which reaches as far back as the formation of the Earth itself, at least 4,700 million years ago.

Here are the names of the four eras which cover the time from the beginning of life to the present day, and the names of the periods which sub-divide them. (Until the Pleistocene era, all the dates are given in millions of years ago, so 'earlier than 597' means more than 597,000,000 years ago!)

| Era | Period | Date | Description and Evolution |
|---|---|---|---|
| Pre-Cambrian (Before the Cambrian era) | | (Millions of years ago. Earlier than 597) | Earliest dated rock formations. |
| Palaeozoic (Age of Ancient Life) | Cambrian | 510 to 596 | Only marine invertebrates (jellyfish and sponges) existed. No animals lived on the land. |
| | Ordovician | 435–460 to 510 | Earliest fish vertebrates appeared and the continents were flooded. |
| | Silurian | 405 to 435–460 | Earliest land plants developed. |
| | Devonian | 360 to 405 | Ancestors of fish and the earliest insects appeared. |
| | Carboniferous | 280 to 360 | Earliest spider, four-footed animals and conifers appeared. |
| | Permian | 235 to 280 | Earliest land reptiles appeared. |
| Mesozoic (Age of Reptiles) | Triassic | 210 to 235 | Dinosaurs first evolved. |
| | Jurassic | 135 to 210 | Earliest gliders and earliest mammals appeared. |
| | Cretaceous | 64 to 135 | Abundant hardwood palms and seed-bearing trees developed. Reptiles replaced dinosaurs. |

| Cenozoic (Age of Mammals) | Palaeocene | 54 to 64 | Ancestors of horse, pig, cow, elephant and rhinoceros appeared. Turtles and tortoises evolved, abundant flowering plants existed. |
| | Eocene | 38 to 54 | Continuation of Palaeocene developments. |
| | Oligocene | 26 to 38 | Increase of plant eating animals. Ancestors of modern cats, dogs and bears appeared. |

| Miocene | 7 to 26 | Primitive manlike ape, long-legged water birds appeared. Europe and Asia joined. |
| Pliocene | 2 to 7 | Manlike apes developed. Marine life similar to today, horses, elephants and other mammals began to have greater resemblance to modern types. |
| Pleistocene | 50,000 BC to 1,750,000 BC | Ice Ages left mammoths and giant mammals, hardy plant varieties in Europe and Stone Age cave men. |
| Holocene | Present to 50,000 BC | Disappearance of the Ice-sheets, all the present forms of mammals were in existence. |

# TEN PREHISTORIC ANIMALS STILL IN EXISTENCE

| Animal | Species | Age |
|---|---|---|
| Australian Lungfish | Fish | 200 million years old |
| Coelacanth | Fish | 400 million years old |
| Crocodile | Reptile | 160–195 million years old |
| Duckbill Platypus | Aquatic Mammal | 150 million years old |
| Horseshoe Crab | Crustacean | 300 million years old |
| Okapi | African Mammal | 30 million years old |
| Peripatus | Worm | 500 million years old |
| Stephens Island Frog | Amphibian | 170–275 million years old |
| Tuatara | Reptile | 200 million years old |
| Turtle | Reptile | 275 million years old |

# THE AGE OF REPTILES

For millions of years, the earth's leading animals were reptiles and the period when they were dominant is called the Age of Reptiles. However, many of the reptiles which were then very common are now extinct. These were some of them:

Dinosaurs – The largest dinosaurs were the biggest animals ever to walk on the earth and their disappearance marked the end of the reptile dominance.

Ichtyosaur – The name means the 'fish reptile' and this animal closely resembles a fish in appearance. The largest Ichtyosaurs were about 7.6 metres long and could swim very well. They were extinct before the end of the Age of Reptiles.

Mosasaurs – These were an ancient form of marine lizard which lasted late into the period. They sometimes grew to a length of 9–12 metres.

Pelyosaurs – Some Pelyosaurs had two enormous fins, like 'sails' growing vertically from their backs which give the impression that they lived in the sea. However, they were land based animals.

Plesiosaurs – These reptiles did live in the sea. They looked rather like modern turtles with broad flat bodies and legs shaped like paddles. Unlike turtles though Plesiosaurs had very long necks with small heads. They became extinct about 70 million years ago and their fossils show that some of them grew to lengths of 15 metres.

Pterosaurs & Pterodactyls – Both of these animals were flying reptiles with large wings. The Pteranodon, last of the Pterosaurs, had a wing span of over 9 metres. However, the flying reptiles left no descendants because modern birds are descended from other reptiles not from Pterosaurs or Pterodactyls as one might expect.

## Q.E.D.

Q.E.D. is an abbreviation. It stands for three Latin words 'quod erat demonstrandum', which mean 'which was to be proved'. Abbreviations are made with many of the other letters in the alphabet and here are some of the more common English ones.

*A*

| | |
|---|---|
| a. | area |
| A.A. | Automobile Association |
| | Anti-Aircraft |
| A.A.A. | Amateur Athletic Association |
| A. and M. (Hymns) | Ancient and Modern |
| A.B. | Able-bodied Seaman |
| A.B.C. | Alphabet |
| | (also Aerated Bread Company) |
| a.c. | alternating current |
| a/c | accounts |
| A.D. | Anno Domini. In the year of our Lord |
| A.D.C. | Aide-de-Camp |
| Ad. lib. | Ad libitum. At pleasure |
| Adm. | Admiral |
| A.F.C. | Air Force Cross |
| A.F.M. | Air Force Medal |
| alt. | altitude |
| a.m. | ante meridiem. Before noon |
| A.M.D.G. | Ad majorem Dei Gloriam. To the greater glory of God. |

| anon. | anonymous |
| A.N.Z.A.C. | Australian and New Zealand Army Corps |
| A.S.A. | Amateur Swimming Association |
| A.S.D.I.C. | Anti-Submarine detector indicator committee |
| A.S.E.A.N. | Association of South-East Asian Nations |
| av. | average |
| A.W.O.L. | Absent Without Leave |

*B*

| b | born; bowled |
| B.A. | Bachelor of Arts |
| B.A.C. | British Aircraft Corporation |
| B.A.O.R. | British Army of the Rhine |
| B.B. | Boys Brigade |
| B.B.C. | British Broadcasting Corporation |
| B.C. | Before Christ |
| B.Ch. (or Ch.B.) | Bachelor of Surgery |
| B.C.L. | Bachelor of Civil Law |
| B.D. | Bachelor of Divinity |
| B.D.A. | British Dental Association |
| B.Ed. | Bachelor of Education |
| B.E.M. | British Empire Medal |
| B.L. | British Leyland |
| B.Litt | Bachelor of Literature, or of Letters |
| B.M.A. | British Medical Association |
| B.N.C. | Brasenose College (Oxon.) |
| B.N.O.C. | British National Oil Corporation |
| b.p. | boiling point |
| B.Phil | Bachelor of Philosophy |
| B.R.C.S. | British Red Cross Society |
| B.Sc. | Bachelor of Science |
| B.S.T. | British Standard Time |
| Bt. | Baronet |

| B.V.M. | Blessed Virgin Mary |
| B.V.M.S. | Bachelor of Veterinary Medicine and Surgery |

### C

| C. | Conservative; Centigrade |
| c. | circa (about) |
| Cantab. | Cambridge |
| Cantuar. | Canterbury |
| cap. | capital letter; capitulum (chapter) |
| C.B. | Companion of the Bath |
| C.B.E. | Commander of Order of British Empire |
| C.B.I. | Confederation of British Industry |
| cc | cubic centimetres |
| C.C.F. | Combined Cadet Force |

| | |
|---|---|
| C.E. | Civil Engineer |
| C.E.N.T.O. | Central Treaty Organisation |
| C.E.T. | Central European Time |
| C. of E. | Church of England |
| cf. | confer. (compare) |
| C.G.M. | Conspicuous Galantry Medal |
| C.H. | Companion of Honour |
| Ch.Ch. | Christ Church |
| C.I. | Channel Islands |
| C.I.A. | Central Intelligence Agency |
| C.I.D. | Criminal Investigation Department |
| C.-in-C. | Commander-in-Chief |
| cm | centimetre(s) |
| C.M.G. | Companion Order of St. Michael and St. George |
| C.O. | Commanding Officer |
| C.O.D. | Cash on Delivery |
| C.O.I. | Central Office of Information |
| C.T.C. | Cyclists' Touring Club |
| cwt. | hundredweight |

*D*

| | |
|---|---|
| d. | daughter, died |
| D.B.E. | Dame Commander of Order of British Empire |
| D.C. | District of Columbia |
| D.C.L. | Doctor of Civil Law |
| D.D. | Doctor of Divinity |
| D. Litt | Doctor of Letters, or of Literature |
| D. Phil | Doctor of Philosophy |
| D.Sc. | Doctor of Science |
| D.C.M. | Distinguished Conduct Medal |
| D.D.T. | dichlorodiphenyltrichloroethane (insecticide) |
| del. | delineavit He (she) drew it. |
| D.F.C. | Distinguished Flying Cross |
| D.F.M. | Distinguished Flying Medal |

| | |
|---|---|
| D.G. | Dei gratia. By the grace of God. |
| DM | Deutsche Mark |
| Do. | Ditto. The same |
| D.V. | Deo volente. God willing |

*E*

| | |
|---|---|
| E. and O.E. | Errors and omissions excepted |
| E.E.C. | European Economic Community |
| E.F.T.A. | European Free Trade Association |
| e.g. | exempli gratia. For the sake of example |
| E.R. | Elizabeth Regina, or Edwardus Rex |
| et. al. | et alibi (and elsewhere); et alii (and others) |
| etc. | et cetera. And the other things |
| et. seq. | et sequentia. And the following |
| ex. lib. | ex libris. From the books of |

*F*

| | |
|---|---|
| F. | Fahrenheit |
| F.A. | Football Association |
| F.B.I. | Federal Bureau of Investigation (U.S.) |
| F.D. | Fidei Defensor. Defender of the Faith |
| F.H. | Fire Hydrant |
| fl. | floruit. He, or she, flourished |
| F.O. | Flying Officer; Foreign Office |
| f.p. | freezing point |

*G*

| | |
|---|---|
| g. | gram(s) |
| G.B.E. | Knight or Dame Grand Cross of British Empire |
| G.C. | George Cross |
| G.C.B. | Knight or Dame Grand Cross of the Bath |

| | |
|---|---|
| G.C.M.G. | Knight or Dame Grand Cross of St. Michael and St. George |
| G.C.V.O. | Knight or Dame Grand Cross of Royal Victorian Order |
| G.D.P. | Gross Domestic Product |
| Gen. | General; Genesis |
| G.H.Q. | General Headquarters |
| G.L.C. | Greater London Council |
| G.M. | George Medal |
| G.M.T. | Greenwich Mean Time |
| G.O.C. | General Officer Commanding |
| G.P.O. | General Post Office |
| G.R. | Georgius Rex, King George |
| G.S.O. | General Staff Officer |

*H*

| | |
|---|---|
| H.C.F. | Highest Common Factor |
| H.E. | His Excellency; His Eminence |
| H.E.H. | His, Her, Exalted Highness |
| H.H. | His, Her, Highness |
| H.I.H. | His, Her, Imperial Highness |
| H.I.M. | His, Her, Imperial Majesty |
| H.M. | His, Her, Majesty |
| H.M.S. | His, Her, Majesty's Ship |
| H.M.S.O. | His, Her, Majesty's Stationery Office |
| H.N.C. | Higher National Certificate |
| h.p. | horse power |
| H.Q. | Headquarters |
| H.R.H. | His, Her, Royal Highness |
| H.S.H. | His, Her, Serene Highness |

*I*

| | |
|---|---|
| I.A.T.A. | International Air Transport Association |
| i.b. (or ibid.) | ibidem (in the same place) |
| i.e. | id est. That is |
| inf. | infinitive |
| inst. | instant. Current month |
| I.O.M. | Isle of Man |

| | |
|---|---|
| I.O.U. | I owe you |
| I.O.W. | Isle of Wight |
| I.Q. | Intelligence Quotient |
| I.T.A. | Independent Television Authority |
| I.T.V. | Independent Television |

*J*

| | |
|---|---|
| J.P. | Justice of the Peace |

*K*

| | |
|---|---|
| K.B.E. | Knight Commander of Order of British Empire |
| K.G. | Knight of the Garter |
| km. | kilometre |
| k.o. | knock out (boxing) |
| K.P. | Knight of St. Patrick |
| K.T. | Knight of the Thistle |
| Kt. | Knight Bachelor |

*L*

| | |
|---|---|
| L. (or Lib.) | Liberal |
| Lab. | Labour |
| lb. | libra. Pound weight |
| l.b.w. | leg before wicket |
| Litt.D. | Doctor of Letters |
| LL.D. | Doctor of Law |
| L S D | Librae, solidi, denarii. Pounds, shillings, pence |
| L.S.O. | London Symphony Orchestra |
| L.T.A. | Lawn Tennis Association |
| Ltd. | Limited Liability |

*M*

| | |
|---|---|
| M. | Member; Monsieur |
| M.A. | Master of Arts |
| M.B.E. | Member of British Empire Order |
| M.C. | Military Cross |
| M.C.C. | Marylebone Cricket Club |

| | |
|---|---|
| M.F.H. | Master of Fox Hounds |
| Mgr. | Monsignor |
| Min. Plenip. | Minister Plenipotentiary |
| Mlle. | Mademoiselle |
| M.M. | Military Medal (also MM., Messieurs) |
| Mme. | Madame |
| M.N. | Merchant Navy |
| M.O.H. | Medical Officer of Health |
| M.P. | Member of Parliament |
| m.p.h. | miles per hour |
| MS. | manuscript |

*N*

| | |
|---|---|
| N.A.A.F.I. | Navy, Army and Air Force Institutes |
| N.A.T.O. | North Atlantic Treaty Organization |
| N.B. | Nota bene. Note well |
| N.C.B. | National Coal Board |
| N.C.O. | Non-commissioned Officer |
| Nem. con. | Nemine contradicente. No one contradicting |
| Net | free from, or not subject to any deductions |
| N.F.U. | National Farmers' Union |
| N.H.S. | National Health Service |
| No. | Numero. Number |
| Non seq. | non sequitur. It does not follow |
| N.S. | Nova Scotia |
| N.S.P.C.C. | National Society for the Prevention of Cruelty to Children |
| N.S.W. | New South Wales |
| N.U.J. | National Union of Journalists |
| N.U.S. | National Union of Students |
| N.U.R. | National Union of Railwaymen |
| N.Y. | New York |

| N.Z. | New Zealand |
|---|---|

*O*

| O.B.E. | Officer of British Empire Order |
|---|---|
| O.C. | Officer Commanding |
| O.E.C.D. | Organization for Economic Co-operation & Development |
| O.E.D. | Oxford English Dictionary |
| O.H.M.S. | On Her Majesty's Service |
| O.M. | Order of Merit (and member of) |
| O.P.E.C. | Organization of Petroleum Exporting Countries |
| op. cit. | opere citato. In the work cited |
| Oxon. | Oxford; Oxfordshire |
| Oz. | Ounce |

*P*

| P.A.Y.E. | Pay as you earn |
|---|---|
| P.C. | Privy Councillor |
| p.c. | post card; per cent |
| P.D.S.A. | People's Dispensary for Sick Animals |
| Ph.D. | Doctor of Philosophy |
| P.L.A. | Port of London Authority |
| P.M. | Post meridiem. Afternoon; Prime Minister |
| P.M.G. | Post Master General |
| p.p. or per pro | per procurationem – by proxy. (pp. = pages also) |
| Pro tem. | pro tempore. For the time being |
| P.S. | Post scriptum, postscript |
| P.T. | Physical Training |
| P.T.O. | Please turn over |

*Q*

| Q.C. | Queen's Counsel |
|---|---|
| Q.e.d. | quod erat demonstrandum. Which was to be proved |

| | |
|---|---|
| Q.G.M. | Queen's Gallantry Medal |
| *R* | |
| R.A. | Royal Artillery or Royal Academy |
| R.A.C. | Royal Armoured Corps (also Royal Automobile Corps) |
| R.A.F. | Royal Air Force |
| R.A.M. | Royal Academy of Music |
| R.A.Mc. | Royal Army Medical Corps |
| R.E. | Royal Engineers |
| R.E.M.E. | Royal Electrical and Mechanical do. |
| R.I.B.A. | Royal Institute of British Architects (also Member of the Institute) |
| R.M. | Royal Marines |
| R.S.P.C.A. | Royal Society for the Prevention of Cruelty to Animals. |
| R.I.P. | Requiescat in pace. May he, she rest in peace |
| r.p.m. | revolutions per minute |
| R.S.V.P. | Répondez s'il vous plait. Answer if you please. |
| *S* | |
| S.E.A.T.O. | South East Asia Treaty Organization |
| S.H.A.P.E. | Supreme Headquarters, Allied Powers, Europe |
| Sic. | So written |
| S.J. | Society of Jesus |
| S.O.S. | Save Our Souls. Distress signal |
| S.P.C.K. | Society for Promoting Christian Knowledge |
| S.P.Q.R. | Senatus Populusque Romanus. The Senate and People of Rome |
| S.R.N. | State Registered Nurse |
| Stet. | Let it stand |
| S.T.D. | Sacrae Theologiae Doctor; Subscriber Trunk Dialling |

*T*

| | |
|---|---|
| T.B. | Tuberculosis |
| T.D. | Territorial Decoration |
| T.N.T. | Trinitrotoluene (explosive) |
| T.U.C. | Trades Union Congress |

*U*

| | |
|---|---|
| U.H.F. | Ultra-high frequency |
| U.K. | United Kingdom |
| U.N.E.S.C.O. | United Nations Educational, Scientific and Cultural Organization |
| U.N.O. | United Nations Organization |
| U.S.A. or U.S. | United States of America |
| U.S.S.R. | Union of Soviet Socialist Republics |

*V*

| | |
|---|---|
| v. | vide (see); versus (against) |
| V.A.T. | Value Added Tax |
| V.C. | Victoria Cross |
| V.H.F. | Very High Frequency |
| V.I.P. | Very Important Person |
| Viz. | Videlicet. Namely |

*W*

| | |
|---|---|
| W.E.U. | Western European Union |
| W.H.O. | World Health Organization |
| W.R.A.C. | Women's Royal Army Corps |
| W.R.A.F. | Women's Royal Air Force |
| W.R.N.S. | Women's Royal Navy Service |
| W.R.V.S. | Women's Royal Voluntary Service |

*Y*

| | |
|---|---|
| Y.M.C.A. | Young Men's Christian Association |
| Y.W.C.A. | Young Women's do. |

Railways

## RAILWAY DEVELOPMENTS

*Date*    *Events and Inventions*
1597    The earliest reference to a wagonway in England
        describes one linking coal mines with the river
        Trent. The wagons were drawn by animals.
1727    The first railway viaduct in England, Tanfield
        Arch, was completed.

1768 Wooden rails began to be replaced by ones made of cast iron.

1769 The first self-moving steam engine was demonstrated. It was built by Nicholas Cugnot, (France).

1782 James Watt invented a steam-engine capable of running on wheels.

1795 The long-brake was invented, allowing a safer descent of steep inclines.

1801 A full-size steam-carriage was invented by Richard Trevithick (UK).

1803 The Surrey Iron Railway, built by William Jessop and James Outram (UK), became the first public freight railway in the world.

1804 The first self-propelled locomotive to run on rails was built by Richard Trevithick to run at Pennydarren, Wales. Unfortunately the engine was too heavy for the rails.

1806 The first railway line to carry fare-paying passengers was opened between Swansea and Oystermouth, Wales. The carriages were pulled by horses.

1810 Wrought-iron rails were introduced.

1814 George Stephenson (UK) built his first steam engine, 'Blutcher'.

1825 The first regularly operated steam railway in the world was opened from Stockton to Darlington. It carried freight exclusively.

1829 Stephenson's locomotive 'Rocket' won the Rainhill Trials, near Liverpool.

1830 The first railway in the USA was opened, the South Carolina Railroad.

1836 The world's first narrow guage railway was opened at Festiniog, Wales.

1837 The first sleeping cars appeared, in Pennsylvania, USA.

1840 Disc and crossbar signals were first introduced in the UK.

1846   Track gauge in the UK was standardised at 4 ft 8½ in (1.453 m).

1854   The first military railway was built during the Crimea War. It ran 20 miles (32.18 km) from Balaclava to the front line.

1855   The first special mail train ran from London to Bristol, England.

1857   The first steel rail was manufactured and laid experimentally at Derby, England.

1863   The first dining cars were introduced on the Baltimore to Philadelphia run in the USA.

1863   The first underground city railway was opened in London, running from Bishop's Gate to Farringdon.

1867   The first elevated railway, running from an experimental overhead track, was built in Manhattan, New York, USA.

1869    The Pacific Railroad, running from coast to coast across the USA, was completed.

1879    The first electric railway was displayed on a 300 yd (274 m) track at the Berlin Trade Exhibition. It was invented and built by Werner von Siemen.

1883    The Orient Express came into service, running from Paris to Istanbul via Vienna.

1885    The Canadian Pacific Railway was completed.

1890    The first electric underground railway was opened in London.

1893    The first electric traction railway was built along the shore of the river Mersey, Liverpool, England.

1895    The first stretch of main-line electrification was installed in a railway tunnel under Baltimore, USA.

1897    Rudolf Diesel constructed the first diesel engine.

1910    Main-line electrification was established in Sweden.

1925    The first diesel-electric locomotive was tested in Canada.

1932    The 'Flying Hamburger' was introduced by the German State Railways as the first regular diesel-electric service.

1948    The first gas-turbine electric locomotive was tested.

1955    A French locomotive became the first to pass the 200 mph speed. Its top speed was 205 mph (330 km/h).

1966    New Tokaido Line was opened by Japanese National Railways. It covered the 515 km journey at a speed averaging 163 km/h.

1977    British Rail's High Speed Train averaged over 160 km/h for a distance of over 160 km for the first time.

# WORLD RAILWAY FACTS

| Busiest: | system | Japanese National Railways | Nearly 17,000,000 people carried each day. |
|---|---|---|---|
| Fastest: | diesel train | British Rail High Speed Train | Reached 230.12 km/h |
| | electric train | U.S. LIMRV (Linear Induction Motor Research Model) | Reached 376.9 km/h |
| | regular service | Osaka-Okayama, Japan | Average speed 166.2 km/h |
| | steam train | British locomotive 'Mallard' | Reached 202 km/h |
| Highest: | railway line | La Cima, Peru | 4,817 m high |
| | railway station | Condor, Bolivia | 4,786 m high |
| Longest: | freight train | Norfolk and Western Railway, USA | Nearly 6 km long |
| | railway line | Moscow-Nakhodka, USSR, (Trans-Siberian) | 9,334 km long |
| | non-stop journey (daily) | Richmond, Virginia – Jacksonville, Florida, USA | 1,060 km long |
| | station platform | Bengal, India | 833 m long |
| | straight section of track | Nullarbor Plain Australia | 478 km long |
| Narrowest: | track gauge | Ravenglass & Eskdale and Romney, Hythe & Dymchurch lines in England | 0.381 m wide |
| Steepest: | track section | Chedde-Servoz, France | Gradient is 1.11 |
| Widest: | track gauge | Indian sub-continent Argentina and Chile | 1.676 m wide |

# THE ORIGINS OF FIFTY SPORTS

Archery – Archaeology indicates the use of the bow as early as 46,000 BC. The sport developed during the 16th century when the bow ceased to be used as a weapon.

Athletics – The ancient Olympic games date back to the 13th century BC, but were abolished in 393 AD. The modern sport was revived in England in the early 19th century.

Badminton – The name is taken from Badminton Hall, Avon, England, where the game became popular around 1870. It may be a development of an old children's game, battledore and shuttlecock.

Baseball – The American game developed from the English game Rounders and was played in England and America in the eighteenth century. The modern rules were written at about 1845.

Basketball – Invented by Dr. J. Naismith in Springfield Massachusetts, USA in 1891.

Billiards – First mentioned in France in 1429. Rubber cushions and slate beds were not added until 1835 and 1836 respectively.

Bobsledding – First developed in Switzerland by an Englishman, W. Smith in 1888.

Boxing – Fist-fighting was introduced into the Olympic games around 686 BC. The modern rules were compiled by the Marquess of Queensbury in 1867.

Bowls – Archaeologists estimate that a form of bowls was played in Egypt about 5,000 BC. Bowling at a target is first recorded in England in the 13th century AD.

Bowling (10 pin) – A German game played in church cloisters in the 12th century gives rise to the German word for 'bowling': 'kegeling'. Modern ten pin bowling developed in the USA about 1840.

Canoeing – The sport of canoeing originated in 1866 when J. Macgregor founded the Royal Canoe Club in England.

Cricket – References to cricket date back to the 13th century. The first recorded game of cricket was played in 1550. The M.C.C. set of laws were first compiled in 1835.

Cycling – The first International race was held in Paris in 1868.

Equestrianism (riding and show jumping) – Horse riding probably dates from Anatolia, (Turkey) at about 1400 BC. The first show jumping events were organised about 1865.

Fencing – A carving on an ancient Egyptian temple shows practice sword fighting with blunted swords, masks and judges. It dates from 1190 BC. During the 15th century, the art of skilful sword-play gave rise to the sport as it is known today.

Fives (Eton) – A game which developed at Eton College and which became so popular that the New Courts were built in 1840.

Football – 'Tsu chu' was a form of football played in ancient China at about 350 BC. There are records of football being played in England in the 12th century but the rules were not codified until an attempt was made at Cambridge University in 1846.

Gliding – The first flight in a glider was made in Yorkshire in 1853.

Golf – The first reference to golf is an Act of Parliament of 1457 which prohibited it being played in places where it interfered with archery practice. The first golf 'club' was founded in Edinburgh in 1744.

Gymnastics – Gymnastics were performed in the ancient civilisations of China, Persia, India and Greece but the modern sport developed during the early 19th century after the opening of an open-air gymnasium in Berlin in 1811.

Hang Gliding – The first successful hang gliding pilot was O. Lilienthal of Germany, who was killed hang gliding in 1896. The sport was revived in 1958 and the first World Championships were held in 1976.

Hockey – The first evidence of the playing of hockey is an ancient Egyptian drawing which dates from 2,000 BC. Descriptions of games similar to hockey date from the 12th century in England. The name 'hockey' became generally used in the 19th century.

Horse Racing – Horse riding dates from about 1,400 BC. There are accounts of races between two horses in the 14th century but the first permanent race course was not established until 1540 at Chester, England.

Ice Hockey – Ice Hockey was first played with a puck at Kingston, Ontario, Canada in 1860. The rules were drawn up in Montreal in 1879.

Ice Skating – The earliest mention of skating on ice is in second century AD Scandinavian literature; the first illustration is a Dutch engraving of 1498. The first skating rink was established in New York in 1858.

Judo – Judo developed in Japan in 1882 from the ancient Japanese martial art of 'Jiu Jisu'.

Lacrosse – The North American Indian game of 'baggataway' was christened 'Lacrosse' by French settlers in the 17th century. The first club was formed in Montreal in 1856.

Lawn Tennis – 'Field Tennis' as opposed to 'Court Tennis' is first mentioned in 1793. The first Tennis club was founded at Leamington in 1872.

Motor-Cycle Racing – The first motor cycle race over one mile was held in Surrey in 1897.

Motor Racing – The first motor race (trail) ran from Paris to Rouen in 1894.

Polo – Polo probably developed in central Asia at about 500 BC. The first description of a match was written by the Persian poet Firdausi at about 600 AD. It was later developed by officers of the British army in India.

Rackets – The origins of the modern Engligh game lie in the early forms of handball played in medieval Europe. The earliest record of a covered court is of one built in Exeter in 1798.

Real-Tennis – Sometimes called Royal Tennis, this game was the fore-runner of the now widespread game of Lawn Tennis. It is thought to have developed from a French game 'le jeu de paume', which was played in monastery cloisters by French monks in the 11th century. The oldest surviving court was built in Paris in 1496.

Roller Skating – A type of roller skate was invented by J. Merlin in Belgium in 1760 but the modern type of four-wheeled skate was developed by an American, J. Plympton in 1863. The first internationally recognised world championship was held in 1937.

Rowing – The sport of rowing probably dates as far back as the rowing boat itself. The earliest race was Doggett's Coat and Badge held on the Thames in 1715. The first races described in England were held at Walton-on-Thames in 1768.

Rugby League – The game originated from a professional breakaway by 21 clubs in the north of England.

Rugby Union – Traditionally the game was invented by a pupil called William Webb Ellis, at Rugby School in 1823. The practice of fielding fifteen players a side was introduced in 1875.

Skate Boarding – The sport developed in the USA in the 1960s and the first championship was staged in 1966. A growing popularity since 1975 has led to widespread interest in the UK; the first motorised boards appeared in 1977.

Skiing – Very early skis, which date from 2,000 BC, have been found in northern Europe. Skiing for fun developed in Norway in the first half of the 19th century, and the first ski races were held near Oslo in 1866.

Snooker – The game was developed from 'black pool' in 1875 by a British army officer, Sir Neville Chamberlain.

Speedway – The first speedway races were held on trotting tracks in the USA in 1910, but the sport became properly established in Australia in 1923. The first world championship was organised in 1936.

Squash Rackets – The game developed out of the older game of rackets and was probably originated by pupils at Harrow School 'knocking up' before they went to play rackets itself. The first championship was held in the USA in 1906.

Swimming – Swimming was practised by ancient warriors as part of their martial skills. An imperial decree issued in Japan in 1603 made swimming compulsory in schools. The earliest swimming-bath was opened in Liverpool in 1828.

Table Tennis – This form of miniature indoor tennis was developed in the middle of the 19th century in England. By the 1890s 'ping pong' had become a world-wide craze.

Volleyball – Volleyball was developed by the Y.M.C.A. movement in the USA in 1895.

Water Polo – The sport originated in the UK at about 1870 but did not become recognised by the Swimming Association of Great Britain until 1885.

Weightlifting – Lifting heavy stones was considered a test of manhood in the ancient world and during the

Middle Ages. The first world championship was held in London in 1891.

Wrestling – Wrestling developed as one of the earliest forms of defence practised by ancient man. There are examples of wrestling in the early civilisations of the Mediterranean, Mesopotamia and China. The International Federation for amateur wrestling was established in 1921.

Yachting – Modern yachting developed in the Netherlands during the 16th century. The earliest yacht club was the Cork Water Club of Ireland, founded in 1720.

# OUTSTANDING INDIVIDUALS IN TEN INTERNATIONAL SPORTS

| Sport | Name and Nation | Achievement |
|---|---|---|
| Boxing | J. Louis (USA) | Longest reigning world champion, 1937–1949. |
| | M. Ali | First man to regain the world heavyweight title twice. |
| Cricket | G. St. A. Sobers (Barbados) | Highest Test match innings, 365 not out against Pakistan in 1958. |
| | J. C. Laker (UK) | Highest number of wickets in a Test match, 19 wickets for 90 runs against Australia in 1956. |
| Football (Association) | R. F. Moore (UK) | Highest number of international appearances, 108 caps for England. |
| | G. J. Bambrick (Ireland) | Highest score by one man in an international match, 6 goals scored against Wales in 1930. |
| Gymnastics | B. Shakhlin (USSR) | Greatest number of individual world titles won by a man, 10 between 1954 and 1964. |
| | L. S. Latynina (USSR) | Greatest number of individual world titles won by a woman, 10 between 1956 and 1964. |
| | N. Comaneci (Romania) | Highest score ever gained in the Olympic Games, seven perfect scores of 10.00 in the 1976 Olympics. |
| Lawn Tennis | R. G. Laver (Australia) | First man to achieve the grand slam twice (winning the Wimbledon, US, Australian and French championships), in 1962 and 1969. |

| | W. C. Renshaw (UK) | Greatest number of men's singles Wimbledon wins, 7 titles (1881–89). |
|---|---|---|
| | H. Willis Moody (USA) | Greatest number of ladies singles wins at Wimbledon, 8 titles (1927–38) |
| Motor Cycling | G. Agostini (Italy) | Greatest number of world championship titles, 15 between 1968 and 1974. |
| | S. M. B. Hailwood (UK) | Greatest number of wins in the Isle of Man TT races, 12 between 1961 and 1967. |
| Motor Racing | J. M. Fangio | Winner of most world championships, 5 (in 1951 and 1954–1957). |
| | J. Y. Stewart (UK) | Winner of most Grand Prix, 27 wins between 1965 and 1973. |
| Skiing | C. Cranz | Greatest number of Alpine skiing championships (for both men and women), 12 between 1934 and 1939. |
| | A. Sailer | Greatest number of titles won by a man, 7 between 1956 and 1958. |
| Speedway | O. Fundin (Sweden) | Only man to win the world championship 5 times, in 1956, 1960, 1961, 1963 and 1967. |
| | B. Bridges (New Zealand) | Made the record number of consecutive appearances in the world championship finals, 17 between 1954 and 1970. |
| Swimming | A. Borg (Sweden) | Greatest number of men's world records, 32 between 1921–1929. |
| | R. Hveger (Denmark) | Greatest number of women's world records, 42 between 1936 and 1942. |

## THE WORLD'S TIME

GMT stands for Greenwich Mean Time, and, since the 1880s, it has been Greenwich that has officially set the time for the world. Countries have Standard Time Zones in which they operate, and some of them are hours ahead of GMT, while some of them are hours behind. Some also have variations in summer time.

| Area | Standard time (difference from GMT in hours) | Summer time (difference from GMT in hours) |
|---|---|---|
| Afghanistan | +4½ | |
| Albania | +1 | +2 |
| Algeria | GMT | |
| Andorra | +1 | |
| Angola | +1 | |
| Antigua | −4 | |
| Argentina | −3 | |
| Australia | | |
| (a) New South Wales, Tasmania, Victoria | +10 | +11 |
| (b) Queensland | +10 | |
| (c) Northern Territory | +9½ | |
| (d) South Australia | +9½ | +10½ |
| (e) Western Australia | +8 | |
| Austria | +1 | |
| Bahamas | −5 | −4 |
| Bahrain | +3 | |
| Bangladesh | +6 | |
| Barbados | −4 | |
| Belgium | +1 | +2 |
| Belize | −6 | |
| Benin | +1 | |
| Bermuda | −4 | −3 |
| Bhutan | +5½ | |
| Bolivia | −4 | |
| Botswana | +2 | |
| Brazil | | |
| (a) East | −3 | |
| (b) West | −4 | |
| (c) Territory of Acre | −5 | |
| Brunei | +8 | |
| Bulgaria | +2 | |
| Burma | +6½ | |
| Burundi | +2 | |
| Cameroon | +1 | |
| Canada | | |
| (a) Newfoundland | −3½ | −2½ |

| Area | Standard time (difference from GMT in hours) | Summer time (difference from GMT in hours) |
|---|---|---|
| (b) Atlantic Zone | −4 | −3 |
| (c) jekastern Zone | −5 | −4 |
| (d) Central Zone | −6 | −5 |
| (e) Mountain Zone | −7 | −6 |
| (f) Pacific Zone | −8 | −7 |
| (g) Yukon Territory: | | |
| Whitehorse and | | |
| Watson Lake | −8 | |
| Dawson City and Mayo | −9 | −8 |
| Cape Verde Islands | −1 | |
| Cayman Islands | −5 | |
| Central African Empire | +1 | |
| Chad | +1 | |
| Chile | −4 | −3 |
| China | | |
| (a) Zone 1 (Urumchi) | +6 | |
| (b) Zone II–IV (Chunking, Lanchow, Peking, Shanghai, Harbin) | +8 | |
| Christmas Island | +7 | |
| Cocos Islands | +6½ | |
| Colombia | −5 | |
| Comoro Islands | +3 | |
| Congo | +1 | |
| Costa Rica | −6 | |
| Cuba | −5 | −4 |
| Cyprus | +2 | +3 (North Cyprus only) |
| Czechoslovakia | +1 | |
| Denmark | +1 | |
| Djibouti | +3 | |
| Dominica | −4 | |
| Dominican Republic | −4 | |
| Ecuador | −5 | |
| Egypt | +2 | +3 |
| El Salvador | −6 | |
| Equatorial Guinea | +1 | |
| Ethiopia | +3 | |
| Falkland Islands | −4 | −3 (Port Stanley) |
| Faröe Islands | GMT | |
| Fiji | +12 | |
| Finland | +2 | |
| France | +1 | +2 |

| Area | Standard time (difference from GMT in hours) | Summer time (difference from GMT in hours) |
|---|---|---|
| French Guiana | −3 | |
| French Polynesia | −10 | |
| Gabon | +1 | |
| Gambia | GMT | |
| Germany, East | +1 | |
| Germany, West | +1 | |
| Ghana | GMT | |
| Gibraltar | +1 | |
| Gilbert Islands | | |
|   Ocean Island | +11 | |
|   Gilbert Islands | +12 | |
|   Phoenix Islands | +11 | |
|   Line Islands | +10 | |
| Greece | +2 | +3 |
| Greenland | | |
|   East | −2 | |
|   West | −3 | |
|   Thule | −4 | |
| Grenada | −4 | |
| Guadeloupe | −4 | |
| Guatemala | −6 | |
| Guinea | GMT | |
| Guinea Bissau | −1 | |
| Guyana | −3¼ | −3 (winter time) |
| Haiti | −5 | |
| Honduras | −6 | |
| Hong Kong | +8 | +9 |
| Hungary | +1 | |
| Iceland | GMT | |
| India | +5½ | |
| Indonesia | | |
|   (a) Western Zone | +7 | |
|   (b) Central Zone | +8 | |
|   (c) Eastern Zone | +9 | |
| Iran | +3½ | |
| Iraq | +3 | |
| Ireland | GMT | +1 |
| Israel | +2 | +3 |
| Italy | +1 | +2 |
| Ivory Coast | GMT | |
| Jamaica | −5 | −4 |
| Japan | +9 | |
| Johnston Island | −11 | |
| Jordan | +2 | +3 |

| Area | Standard time (difference from GMT in hours) | Summer time (difference from GMT in hours) |
|---|---|---|
| Kampuchea | +7 | |
| Kenya | +3 | |
| Korea, North | +9 | |
| Korea, South | +9 | |
| Kuwait | +3 | |
| Laos | +7 | |
| Lebanon | +2 | +3 |
| Lesotho | +2 | |
| Liberia | GMT | |
| Libya | +2 | |
| Liechtenstein | +1 | |
| Luxembourg | +1 | +2 |
| Macao | +8 | +9 |
| Madagascar | +3 | |
| Malawi | +2 | |
| Malaysia | | |
|   (a) Peninsular mainland | $+7\frac{1}{2}$ | |
|   (b) Sabah, Sarawak | +8 | |
| Maldives | +5 | |
| Mali | GMT | |
| Malta | +1 | +2 |
| Martinique | −4 | |
| Mauretania | GMT | |
| Mauritius | +4 | |
| Mexico | −6 | |
|   (a) Mexico City | | |
|   (b) Baja California Sur, States of Sonora, Sinaloa, Nayarit | −7 | |
| Mongolia | $+7\frac{1}{2}$ | |
| Morocco | GMT | |
| Mozambique | +2 | |
| Namibia | +2 | |
| Nauru | $+11\frac{1}{2}$ | |
| Nepal | +5.40 minutes | |
| Netherlands | +1 | |
| Netherlands Antilles | −4 | |
| New Caledonia | +11 | |
| New Hebrides | +12 | |
| New Zealand | +12 | +13 |
| Nicaragua | −6 | |
| Niger | +1 | |
| Nigeria | +1 | |
| Niue | +11 | |
| Norway | +1 | |

| Area | Standard time (difference from GMT in hours) | Summer time (difference from GMT in hours) |
|---|---|---|
| Oman | +4 | |
| Pakistan | +5 | |
| Panama | −5 | |
| Papua New Guinea | +10 | |
| Paraguay | −4 | −3 |
| Peru | −5 | |
| Philippines | +8 | |
| Pitcairn Island | −9 | |
| Poland | +1 | |
| Portugal | +1 | |
| Qatar | +3 | |
| Reunion | −4 | |
| Rhodesia | +2 | |
| Rumania | +2 | |
| Rwanda | +2 | |
| Sahara Western | GMT | +1 |
| Saint Helena | GMT | |
| St. Kitts-Nevis, Anguilla | −4 | |
| Samoa, American | +11 | |
| Samoa, Western | +11 | |
| São-Tomé and Principe | GMT | |
| Saudi Arabia | +3 | |
| Senegal | GMT | |
| Seychelles | +4 | |
| Sierra Leone | GMT | |
| Singapore | +7½ | |
| Somalia | +3 | |
| South Africa | +2 | |
| Spain | +1 | +2 |
| Sri Lanka | +5½ | |
| Sudan | +2 | |
| Surinam | −3½ | |
| Swaziland | +2 | |
| Sweden | +1 | |
| Switzerland | +1 | |
| Syria | +2 | +3 |
| Taiwan | +8 | +9 |
| Tanzania | +3 | |
| Thailand | +7 | |
| Timor, East | +8 | |
| Togo | GMT | |
| Tonga | +13 | |
| Trinidad and Tobago | −4 | |
| Tunisia | +1 | |

| Area | Standard time (difference from GMT in hours) | Summer time (difference from GMT in hours) |
|---|---|---|
| Turkey | +2 | +3 |
| Turks and Caicos Islands | −5 | |
| Tuvalu | +12 | |
| Uganda | +3 | |
| United Arab Emirates | +4 | |
| United States | | |
|   (a) Eastern Zone | −5 | −4 |
|   (b) Central Zone | −6 | −5 |
|   (c) Mountain Zone | −7 | −6 |
|   (d) Pacific Zone | −8 | −7 |
|   (e) Alaska (Ketchikan to Skagway) | −8 | −7 |
|   (f) Skagway to 141°W | −9 | −8 |
|   (g) 141°W to 162°W | −10 | −9 |
|   (h) 162°W to Westernmost Point | −11 | −10 |
|   (i) Hawaii | −10 | |
| Upper Volta | GMT | |
| Uruguay | −3 | |
| USSR | | |
|   (a) Kiev, Leningrad, Moscow, Odessa | +3 | |
|   (b) Archangel, Volograd, Tbilisi | +4 | |
|   (c) Ashkhabad, Sverdlovsk | +5 | |
|   (d) Alma-Ata, Karaganda, Omsk | +6 | |
|   (e) Novosibirsk, Krasnoyarsk | +7 | |
|   (f) Irkutsck | +8 | |
|   (g) Yakutsk | +9 | |
|   (h) Khabarovsk, Vladivostok | +10 | |
|   (i) Magadan, Yuzhno-Sakhalinsk | +11 | |
|   (j) Petropavlovsk-Kamchatskiy | +12 | |
|   (k) Anadyr | +13 | |
| Venezuela | −4 | |
| Vietnam | +7 | |
| Virgin Islands – British | −4 | |
| Virgin Islands – US | −4 | |
| Yemen, North | +3 | |
| Yemen, South | +3 | |
| Yugoslavia | +1 | |
| Zaire | | |
|   (a) Kinshasa, Mbandaka | +1 | |
|   (b) Shaba, Kasai, Kivu | +2 | |
| Zambia | +2 | |

UPUP & away

## IMPORTANT DATES IN AVIATION HISTORY

| Date | Event |
|------|-------|
| 1709 | First ascent by hot air balloon, Portugal. |
| 1785 | First balloon crossing of the English Channel by J. Blanchard (France) and J. Jeffries (USA). |
| 1852 | Flight of first navigable airship, France. |
| 1900 | First Zepplin flight, Germany. |
| 1903 | Orville and Wilbur Wright made the first sustained controlled flights in a powered aircraft, USA. |

1908     First officially recognised aeroplane flight in
          UK made by S. Cody at Farnborough,
          Hampshire.

1909     Louis Bleriot (France) became the first man to
          cross the English Channel by aeroplane.

1912     F. McClean flew a biplane under all the bridges
          over the River Thames in London.

| 1913 | Lt. Nesterov (Russia) was the first man to loop-the-loop. |
|---|---|
| 1913 | The first four-engined plane was flown. |
| 1918 | The Royal Air Force was formed. |
| 1919 | Alcock and Brown completed the first non-stop trans-Atlantic flight. |
| 1919 | The Smith brothers (Australia) made the first flight from England to Australia. |
| 1925–6 | First flight from London to Cape Town and return made by A. Cobham. |
| 1926 | First flight from UK to Australia and return. |
| 1927 | Lindbergh made first solo non-stop crossing of the Atlantic. |
| 1928 | Inauguration of the Flying Doctor Service in Australia. |
| 1929 | First round the world flight by airship. |
| 1929 | R. Byrd made the first flight over the South Pole. |
| 1930 | Amy Johnson became the first woman to fly solo from England to Australia. |
| 1930 | Crash of the airship R101 ended the development of airships in UK. |
| 1936 | First flight by twin-rotor helicopter, Focke-Wuli FW 61. |
| 1939 | Flight of the first jet-propelled aircraft, the Heinkel HE 178. |
| 1941 | H. Dittmar flew at 1,004 km/h in a Messerschmitt ME 163, the first operational rocket-powered fighter in the world. |
| 1947 | C. Yeager (USA) made the first supersonic flight. |
| 1949 | First flight of the De Havilland Comet, the first commercial jet aircraft. |
| 1953 | British European Airways commenced the world's first service by turbo-prop airliner using the Vickers Viscount. |
| 1968 | First supersonic transport flown, the Russian Tupolev TU-144. |

| 1969 | First flight of the Anglo-French supersonic airliner, Concorde. |
| 1970 | First trans-Atlantic flight by Boeing 747 'Jumbo Jet'. |
| 1976 | Concorde began scheduled air services with British Airways and Air France. |
| 1977 | First cheap fare trans-Atlantic Skytrain operated by Laker Airways. |
| 1978 | First successful crossing of the Atlantic by three American balloonists. |

# TEN OF THE WORLD'S FASTEST AIRCRAFT

| Type | Name | Speed (in km/h) |
|------|------|-----------------|
| Airliner | Tu-144 (USSR) | 2,550 |
| Autogyro | Wa-116 (UK) | 179 |
| Biplane | Fiat C.R.42B. (Italy) | 520 |
| Bomber | Dassault Mirage IV (France) | 2,333 |
| Fighter | Mikoyan MiG-25 (USSR) | 2,975 |
| Flying Boat | Martin XP6M-1 (USA) | 1,040 |
| Jet | Lockheed SR-71A (USA) | 3,529.56 |
| Piston-engined aeroplane | Hawker 'Sea Fury' (USA) | 836 |
| Propeller-driven aeroplane | Tu 114 (USSR) | 877 |
| Rocket-propelled aircraft | X-15A-2 (USA) | 7,297 |

(It is estimated that the Rockwell International Space Shuttle Orbiter will reach 28,325 km/h when it is put into service flying outside the atmosphere.)

## Vehicles

# IMPORTANT DATES IN MOTORING HISTORY

1770   The first genuine automobile was built by N.
       Cugnot, powered by steam.
1801   The first steam carriage in Britain was built by
       R. Trevithick.
1861   The Locomotives Act instituted a speed limit of
       10 mph (16.09 km/h) in the country and half
       that speed in the towns and made it obligatory
       for two people to be in charge of all motor
       vehicles.

1865   The Locomotives Act reduced the speed limit to 4 mph (6.43 km/h), 2 mph (3.21 km/h) in towns, increased the crew of mechanically propelled vehicles to three and stated that one of them should walk not less than six yards (5.4 m) in front of the vehicle carrying a red flag by day and a lantern at night.

1885   Daimler and Benz separately designed the first practical internal combustion engine.

1894   Road racing began in France.

1895   The first practical motor-car tyre was produced by Michelin in France.

The first British motor show was held at Tunbridge Wells.

1896    Speeds of up to 14 mph (22.53 km/h) became legal in the UK; the flag carrier was abolished.

Ford built his first car in the USA.

1897    The RAC was founded by R. Sims.

1903    The Motor Car Act raised the speed limit to 20 mph (32.18 km/h), made provision for driving licences and made registration and number plates compulsory.

1905    The AA was founded.

1908    The first model T Ford, the 'Tin Lizzie' was produced.

1910    Tax on petrol was introduced at a rate of 3d per gallon.

1919    The price of petrol had risen to 4 shillings a gallon from the pre-war cost of 1/9d.

1920    The first roadside petrol pump in Britain was installed near Newbury, Berkshire.

1923    The first British victory in a Grand Prix was won by H. Seagrave driving a Sunbeam.

1930    The 20 mph speed limit was abolished.

1934    The New Road Traffic Act set a speed limit of 30 mph in built-up areas, in the UK.

| 1937 | The London Motor Show was held at Earl's Court for the first time. |
|------|------|
| 1939 | Petrol rationing was introduced in the UK. |
| 1950 | Petrol rationing was abolished in the UK. The tubeless tyre was developed in the USA. |
| 1955 | The first Highway Code appeared in the UK. |
| 1957 | The 40 mph (64.37 km/h) speed limit was introduced experimentally and was confirmed a year later. |
| 1958 | The first stretch of motorway in the UK was opened near Preston. |
| 1960 | Traffic wardens were first appointed in the UK. The 50 mph (80.46 km/h) speed limit was introduced and confirmed in 1961 for 'main' roads. |
| 1965 | The experimental overall speed limit of 70 mph (112.65 km/h) was introduced, becoming law in 1967. |
| 1967 | The breath test was introduced into the UK. |
| 1969 | The fitting of seat belts became compulsory in cars registered on or after January 1, 1965. |
| 1974 | The following speed limits were introduced to control fuel consumption in the UK: 70 mph (112.65 km/h) on motorways. 60 mph (96.55 km/h) on dual carriageways. 50 mph (80.46 km/h) on single carriageways. |
| 1977 | Speed limits were restored to their 1965 levels. |
| 1977 | The wearing of seat belts was made compulsory in Northern Ireland. |

## MOTOR RACING

Club Racing – Competitions for all types of racing cars from Vintage Sports Cars to modern Formula cars. These rank as 'testing grounds' for new drivers.

Drag Racing – Originally an American sport this has become increasingly popular in Europe in recent years. The competition lies in covering a short distance in a straight line in the shortest time.

Grand Prix – This is track racing designed only for true 'racing cars' which decides the World Championship.

Rallies – Competitions which involve a variety of driving skills as well as physical and mechanical endurance over long distances are called 'rallies'. The winners of the various sections are those who lose the fewest amount of points.

Road Racing – Originally driven on normal roads, most of these events are now held on closed circuits, as is the case with the famous 'Le Mans' race. There are competitions open to all classes of sports and racing cars.

Time Trials – Many different events are included in this category where the drivers are set to achieve the fastest time driving 'against the clock'. Some of the most common Time Trials are hill climbs, rally cross and sprint events.

Track Racing – Pure racing cars are divided into Formulae for track racing:

Formula 1 – for single seater cars with 1–3 litres engines unsupercharged, or $1\frac{1}{2}$ litres supercharged. The maximum number of cylinders is twelve.

Formula 2 – for single seater cars with engines up to 2 litres. Superchargers are not allowed and the maximum number of cylinders is restricted to six.

Formula 3 – 2 litres capacity for modifications to cars of which more than 5,000 are manufactured.

Among the other formulae that exist, Formula Ford, based on cars powered by Ford engines, and Formula 5,000 for big-engined cars, are two of the most popular.

Track Racing – also includes events for production cars and Vintage or Veteran cars.

Trials – These events held over difficult driving conditions in winter, test the skills of the driver and the team who prepare and maintain the car. The driver who gets the farthest along the course is the winner.

# MODERN PRODUCTION CARS

| | | |
|---|---|---|
| Fastest | Lamborghini Countach, and Aston Martin Lagonda *Bulldog* | 300 km/h |
| Heaviest | Z11 114 (USSR) | 3,175 kg |
| Largest Engine Capacity | Cadillac Fleetwood Eldorado | 8,195 cc |
| Least Expensive | Fiat 126 | £1,990 |
| Longest | Checker Areobus Limousine | 6.85 m |
| Most Expensive | Rolls Royce Camargue | £79,160 |
| Most Produced | Volkswagen Beetle | 19,200,000 until production in West Germany ceased in 1978. |

Water, Water, Every where

# THE FOUR OCEANS

|          | Area (km²)   | Greatest depth (m) |
|----------|--------------|--------------------|
| Pacific  | 165,240,000  | 10,900             |
| Atlantic | 82,360,000   | 8,381              |
| Indian   | 73,550,000   | 8,046              |
| Arctic   | 26,600,000   | 5,424              |

## THE WORLD'S TOP TEN SEAS

|                   | Area (km²)  | Average depth (m) |
|-------------------|-------------|-------------------|
| Malay Sea         | 8,142,000   | 1,200             |
| Caribbean Sea     | 2,753,000   | 2,400             |
| Mediterranean Sea | 2,503,000   | 1,485             |
| Bering Sea        | 2,268,180   | 1,400             |
| Gulf of Mexico    | 1,542,985   | 5,000             |
| Sea of Okhotsk    | 1,527,570   | 840               |
| East China Sea    | 1,249,150   | 180               |
| Hudson Bay        | 1,232,300   | 120               |
| Sea of Japan      | 1,007,500   | 1,370             |
| Andaman Sea       | 797,700     | 865               |

## THE WORLD'S TOP TEN RIVERS

These are the twenty longest rivers in the world.

| River                          | Outflow        | Length (in km) |
|--------------------------------|----------------|----------------|
| Nile                           | Mediterranean  | 6,670          |
| Amazon                         | Atlantic       | 6,448          |
| Missouri-Mississippi-Red Rock  | Gulf of Mexico | 5,970          |
| Yenisey-Algara-Selenga         | Arctic         | 5,540          |
| Yangtze Kiang                  | North Pacific  | 5,530          |
| Ob'Irtysh                      | Arctic         | 5,410          |
| Hwang Ho                       | North Pacific  | 4,830          |
| Zaire                          | Atlantic       | 4,700          |
| Lena-Kirenga                   | Arctic         | 4,400          |
| Amur-Argun'                    | North Pacific  | 4,345          |

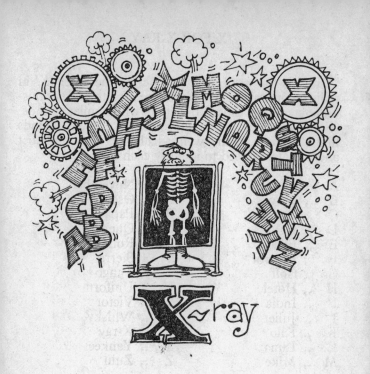

X-ray

# X FOR X-RAY

'X-ray' is the word used to describe the letter 'X' in radio communications. Words are used to prevent misunderstandings caused by letters with similar sounds. (For example, a spoken 'm' sounds like 'n', 'd' sounds like 't'.) These are the twenty-six letters of the alphabet and the words used to identify each one.

| | | | | | |
|---|---|---|---|---|---|
| A | for | Alpha | N | for | November |
| B | ,, | Bravo | O | ,, | Oscar |
| C | ,, | Charlie | P | ,, | Papa |
| D | ,, | Delta | Q | ,, | Quebec |
| E | ,, | Echo | R | ,, | Romeo |
| F | ,, | Foxtrot | S | ,, | Sierra |
| G | ,, | Golf | T | ,, | Tango |
| H | ,, | Hotel | U | ,, | Uniform |
| I | ,, | India | V | ,, | Victor |
| J | ,, | Juliet | W | ,, | Whisky |
| K | ,, | Kilo | X | ,, | X-ray |
| L | ,, | Lima | Y | ,, | Yankee |
| M | ,, | Mike | Z | ,, | Zulu |

## THE MORSE CODE

The Morse code is a method of communication in which letters and numbers are represented by 'dots and dashes'. You can signal in Morse code by flashing a light, by sound or by waving a flag; the dots should be as short as possible and the dashes should be three times as long as the dots.

Over the page you will see Morse code for the different letters of the alphabet, and for punctuation.

| | |
|---|---|
| A ·— | N —· |
| B —··· | O ——— |
| C —·—· | P ·——· |
| D —·· | Q ——·— |
| E · | R ·—· |
| F ··—· | S ··· |
| G ——· | T — |
| H ···· | U ··— |
| I ·· | V ···— |
| J ·——— | W ·—— |
| K —·— | X —··— |
| L ·—·· | Y —·—— |
| M —— | Z ——·· |

| | |
|---|---|
| 1 ·———— | 6 —···· |
| 2 ··——— | 7 ——··· |
| 3 ···—— | 8 ———·· |
| 4 ····— | 9 ————· |
| 5 ····· | 10 ————— |

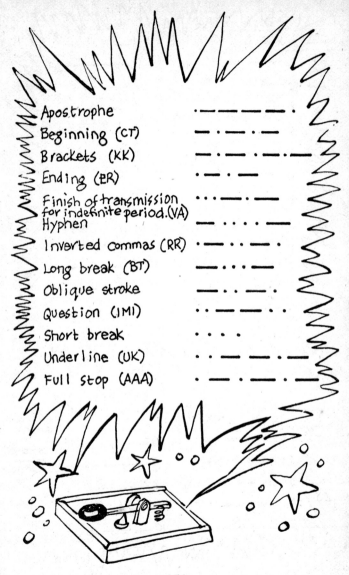

| | |
|---|---|
| Apostrophe | ·————· |
| Beginning (CT) | —·—·— |
| Brackets (KK) | —·——·— |
| Ending (ER) | ·—·—· |
| Finish of transmission for indefinite period.(VA) | ···—·— |
| Hyphen | —····— |
| Inverted commas (RR) | ·—··—· |
| Long break (BT) | —···— |
| Oblique stroke | —··—· |
| Question (IMI) | ··——·· |
| Short break | ·—·—· |
| Underline (UK) | ··——·— |
| Full stop (AAA) | ·—·—·— |

# SEMAPHORE

Semaphore is a means of signalling by holding flags in various positions to indicate letters or numerals. If you make a mistake, use the 'annul' sign to cancel the word. Always make the 'numeral' sign before you signal a number, and give the 'alphabetical' sign when you return to giving letters. Use the letter 'A' to acknowledge each word to show that you understand it.

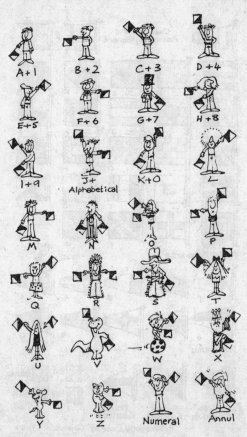

The International Code enables ships to communicate with each other even if the crews speak different languages. There is one flag for every letter of the alphabet and one pennant for each of the ten numerals, and the set is completed by three substitute flags (used when you want to repeat a letter) and the answering or code pennant.

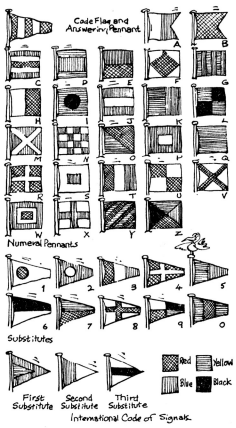

Code Flag and Answering Pennant

Numeral Pennants

Substitutes

First Substitute   Second Substitute   Third Substitute

Red   Yellow   Blue   Black

International Code of Signals

# INTERNATIONAL VEHICLE REGISTRATION LETTERS

When a vehicle is travelling in a country other than its own, it must carry a plate indicating its country of origin. The plate will bear one, two or three letters.

153

| | |
|---|---|
| A | Austria |
| ADN | Southern Yemen |
| AFG | Afghanistan |
| AL | Albania |
| AND | Andorra |
| AUS | Australia |
| B | Belgium |
| BDS | Barbados |
| BG | Bulgaria |
| BH | Belize |
| BR | Brazil |
| BRG | Guyana |
| BRN | Bahrain |
| BRU | Brunei |
| BS | Bahamas |
| BUR | Burma |
| C | Cuba |
| CDN | Canada |
| CGO | Zaire |
| CH | Switzerland |
| CI | Ivory Coast |
| CL | Sri Lanka |
| CO | Colombia |
| CR | Costa Rica |
| CS | Czechoslovakia |
| CY | Cyprus |
| D | Germany |
| DK | Denmark |
| DOM | Dominican Republic |
| DY | Benin |
| DZ | Algeria |
| E | Spain (incl. African localities and provinces) |
| EAK | Kenya |
| EAT | Tanzania |
| EAU | Uganda |
| EAZ | Tanzania |
| EC | Ecuador |
| ET | Egypt |
| F | France (incl. overseas departments and territories) |
| FL | Liechtenstein |
| GB | United Kingdom of Great Britain and Northern Ireland |
| GBA | Alderney |
| GBG | Guernsey Channel Islands |
| GBJ | Jersey |

| GBM | Isle of Man |
| GBZ | Gibraltar |
| GCA | Guatemala |
| GH | Ghana |
| GR | Greece |
| H | Hungary |
| HK | Hong Kong |
| HKJ | Jordan |
| I | Italy |
| IL | Israel |
| IND | India |
| IR | Iran |
| IRL | Ireland (Republic of) |
| IRQ | Iraq |
| IS | Iceland |

| | |
|---|---|
| J | Japan |
| JA | Jamaica |
| K | Kampuchea |
| KWT | Kuwait |
| L | Luxembourg |
| LAO | Laos |
| LB | Liberia |
| LS | Lesotho |
| M | Malta |
| MA | Morocco |
| MC | Monaco |
| MEX | Mexico |
| MS | Mauritius |
| MW | Malawi |
| N | Norway |
| NA | Netherlands Antilles |
| NIC | Nicaragua |
| NIG | Niger |
| NL | Netherlands |
| NZ | New Zealand |
| P | Portugal (incl. Angola, Cape Verde Islands, Mozambique, Portuguese Guinea, Portuguese Timor, São Tomé and Principe) |
| PA | Panama |
| PAK | Pakistan |
| PE | Peru |
| PI | Philippines |
| PL | Poland |
| PTM | Malaysia |
| PY | Paraguay |
| R | Rumania |
| RA | Argentina |
| RB | Botswana |
| RC | Taiwan |
| RCA | Central African Empire |
| RCB | Congo |
| RCH | Chile |
| RH | Haiti |
| RI | Indonesia |
| RIM | Mauritania |
| RL | Lebanon |
| RM | Madagascar |
| RMM | Mali |
| RNR | Zambia |
| ROK | Korea (Republic of) |
| RSM | San Marino |

| | |
|---|---|
| RSR | Rhodesia |
| RU | Burundi |
| RWA | Rwanda |
| S | Sweden |
| SD | Swaziland |
| SF | Finland |
| SGP | Singapore |
| SME | Surinam |
| SN | Senegal |
| SU | Union of Soviet Socialist Republics |
| SUD | Sudan |
| SWA | Namibia (South-West Africa) |
| SY | Seychelles |
| SYR | Syria |
| T | Thailand |
| TG | Togo |
| TN | Tunisia |
| TR | Turkey |
| TT | Trinidad and Tobago |
| U | Uruguay |
| USA | United States of America |
| V | Vatican City (Holy See) |
| VN | Vietnam |
| WAG | Gambia |
| WAL | Sierra Leone |
| WAN | Nigeria |
| WD | Dominica ⎫ |
| WG | Grenada ⎬ Windward Islands |
| WL | St. Lucia ⎭ |
| WS | Western Samoa |
| WV | St. Vincent (Windward Islands) |
| YU | Yugoslavia |
| YV | Venezuela |
| ZA | South Africa |

CD stands for
*Corps Diplomatique*

**ALPHABETS.**

'Z' is the last letter of the Roman alphabet, which we use, but it is not the last letter of every alphabet in the world. There are at least sixty alphabets used in the world, but these are the most common, after our own:

**GREEK**

**ARABIC**

## CYRILLIC

## HEBREW

## THE WORLD'S TOP TEN LANGUAGES

| Language | Number of speakers |
|---|---|
| Guoyu (Mandarin Chinese) | 670,000,000 |
| English | 369,000,000 |
| Russian | 246,000,000 |
| Spanish | 225,000,000 |
| Hindi | 218,000,000 |
| Arabic | 134,000,000 |
| Portuguese | 133,000,000 |
| Bengali | 131,000,000 |
| German | 120,000,000 |
| Japanese | 113,000,000 |